TERRIBLE TIMES

MY STORY
by Tim Witherspoon and Ryan Danes

Published by
Eye-Imagine Publishing Ltd
145-157 ST John Street
London
England
EC1V 4PW

www.eyeimaginepublishing.com

© Tim Witherspoon, 2014

Tim Witherspoon has asserted his rights in accordance with the Copyright, Designs and Patents Act 1988 to be identified as the author of this work. All rights reserved. No part of this publication may be reproduced, stored in a retrieval system, or transmitted in any form or by any means, electronic, mechanical, photocopying, recording or otherwise, without the prior permission in writing of the publisher and the copyright owners, or as expressly permitted by law, or under terms agreed with the appropriate reprographics rights organisation. Enquiries concerning reproduction outside the terms stated here should be sent to the publishers at the UK address printed on this page.

The publisher makes no representation, express or implied, with regard to the accuracy of the information contained in this book and cannot accept any legal responsibility for any errors or omissions that may be made.
A CIP catalogue record for this book is available from the British Library.

First published and printed in 2014
First published in eBook format in 2014

ISBN 978-0-9930942-0-0

The statements and opinions contained in this publication are solely those of Tim Witherspoon and do not necessarily reflect those of the editors or the publisher.

Cover design by Olavi Sona

Printed by
Deltor Communicatuions Ltd
Long Acre
Saltash
Cornwall
England
PL12 6LZ

Acknowledgements

With thanks to: Kevin Baker, Rose Coombes, Rick Cowdery
The Danes and Duncanson families, Deltor, Julie Eaton,
Greg Lambert, The Lancaster Guardian, Keith McMenamin,
Rebecca Rowell, Talliah and Seraya,
The Morecambe Visitor, Andrew Touchstone,
and Murad Ziyad.

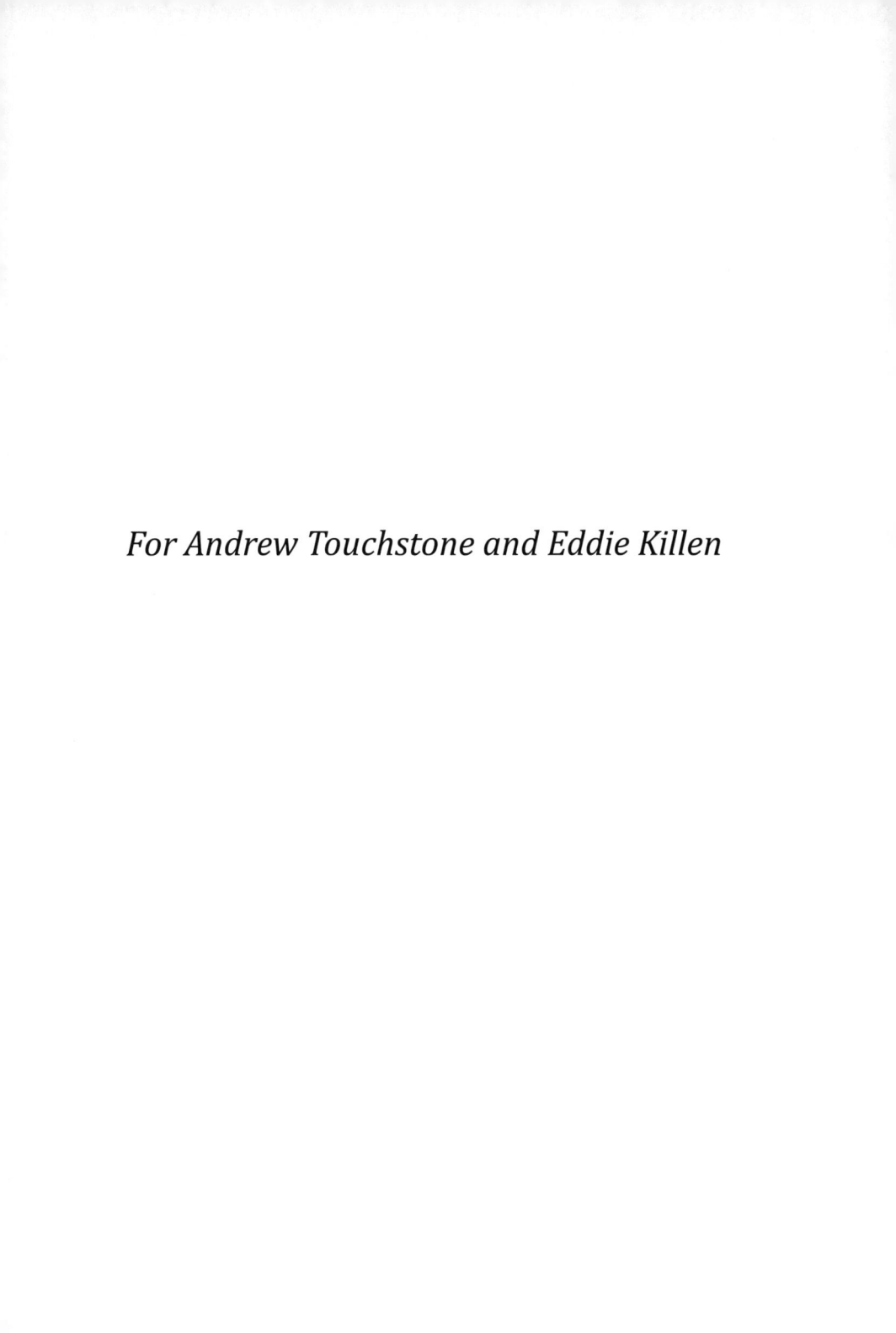

For Andrew Touchstone and Eddie Killen

Contents

1: Born and Raised 1
2: Mighty Crusaders 13
3: Mob-handed 25
4: Doctor Snow 35
5: The Pros and the Cons 47
6: On the Road 57
7: Rising Up 67
8: Looking at Larry. 77
9: The King and the Champion 89
10: Think Pink 101
11: Turning the Screw 133
12: On the Way...to Rehab 147
13: Frank Bruno 157
14: Throwing the Title 169
15: Terrible Times 181
16: Pay-check Fighting 193
17: Ducking and Diving 203
18: End of the Terrible 215
Appendix: *List of fights* 226

Chapter One

Born and Raised

THERE was nothing special at all going on in Philadelphia on December 27, 1957, except for the fact that I was coming into the world. Philadelphia is where I have spent most of my life. I was raised on Emily Street and Seventh, close to where the mafia boss Angelo Bruno was assassinated in March 1980. People called him "The Gentle Don" – he would never let the family get involved in narcotics – and he was killed three blocks away from where I lived in South Philadelphia. The neighborhood I grew up in was mixed; you had a large population of Italians on the higher streets from around Ninth to Twenty-something and you had the Irish on Fourth to Zero, or "Front Street", as they call it. Angelo had been running things since the end of the 1950s and he was seen as the most powerful mafia boss outside of the big cities of New York and Chicago, but he was destined to meet the most terrible end, which seems to be where many of these guys end up.

All us black families were housed in the middle between the Irish and the Italians, so you can imagine we got between lots of business which was nothing to do with us. And, of course, these were the days when blacks were still treated like second-class citizens. Martin Luther King had just founded the Southern Christian Leadership Conference when I was born, and they were fighting for their civil rights. From first grade to eighth, I had to go to school in an Irish neighborhood and we didn't go in on St Patrick's Day. If we did, we would go in groups of a hundred, with our parents walking us to and from the schoolyard. There was also the Emily Street Gang, who were bad dudes; if you wanted a fight, they would certainly give you one. From ninth to twelfth grade, I went to school in an Italian neighborhood and some of those families were connected.

They say that Angelo Bruno's death came about because a couple of his guys betrayed him. He had been in control for more than 20 years and was 69 years old at the time of his death and I guess they wanted new blood. We were outside when we heard the shotgun shell go off, but we didn't know what it was at the time. It was within walking distance and we heard the police cars going up there; my grandma lived right around the corner. My friend Vinnie Burgess, who went on to be a national boxing champion, was coming back from roller-skating with a couple of his friends. A taxi dropped them off on the corner just after it happened and they saw the body. Angelo lived between Ninth and Tenth on Snyder Avenue, and I lived on Fifth. If you check into all the stories about Philly and the mob, you will see more about this, which all happened in our neighborhood. The body of the man who was supposed to have ordered the hit, Antonio Caponigro, was found a few weeks later in the trunk of a car in New York City with about $300 worth of bills stuffed in his mouth and his ass, as a symbol of his greed. They shot Bruno in the face with a shotgun and all the pictures of his corpse are with his mouth open as he is sat in his car; it was not a very dignified way to die. That was where I grew up, south of City Hall and Philly. They called Angelo a good guy, and I used to see him sometimes when I was walking by his house to get to South Philly High School, which I attended. Recalling these memories takes me straight back to the day my brother Stevie got stabbed in the eye, and he was lucky not to lose it. When they found the kid who did it, they threw him down the steps. I made the football team at South Philly and we trained at 12th and Bigler; to get to school we had to risk going up South Broad Street, and you never knew exactly what was going to happen when you were out on the streets. All I can say is that we really must have wanted to play football and baseball.

My dad was Charles Witherspoon but people generally called him "Punchy" because of what he could do with his fists. One of the reasons I didn't put pressure on him about certain things, like why he wasn't around, was because that pain made me as a man, and as a boxer. All my pent-up anger and aggression came from my past, I guess, although I wouldn't say I was a damaged kid.

It was hard for a black man in America back then – I was looking at it that way – and they were scary times to live in, but we didn't know anything else so I can't say I was really affected by it all. It was bad when I was little, and I still see the same people that used the N-word today. They look at me, or give me hugs, and they say "Sorry" but they didn't know any different back then; that's just the way it was. I'm not saying it was alright, but that is the way people lived when I was little. I have an Irish friend who I used to play football with. I saw him a couple of years back, and we sat down in this pub in America and had a drink – he used to call us the N-word, too. What he said to me was that he was sorry, he honestly didn't know what he was saying because he was young and really didn't know any different. Now, when you go into my neighborhood, it's multicultural; you see the whites and the blacks together, and that's the way it should be. I tend to judge people by whether they are good, or bad, not by the color of their skin.

My dad Punchy was a hard-hitting heavyweight. Sometimes they call you by that name because you get hit a lot, but that wasn't the case with my old man. All my uncles were heavyweights; they were called Galloway, Lawrence, Henry, Toot, and O'Neill. There were seven of them originally, including my father, and one of them died when he was about five years old. They always used to be on the corner, street-boxing, or body-boxing, and nobody messed with those guys. Another of my uncles died when he got lynched inside a jailhouse in south Carolina. They took him and hung him. I originally thought they took him off of the street and hung him in the woods; that was the story I remembered from being a kid. One day, some jewellery went missing and they blamed my uncle; after they killed him, it turned up. Nowadays, it's a lot different; I can use my 40 acres and my mule like they were supposed to give to all former slaves in 1865. Down south today, the numbers that are extreme racists are really low. You can't ignore it, of course; you just beware. It's still going on in Philly. A couple of years ago, there were what they were calling 'flash-mobs' out on the street, and it isn't only the whites who are doing it now.

My mother stuck with us through everything. She kept us together, and she told me the truth about my uncle's hanging. She's a doctor of theology now, but she was an electrocardiography technician in the 1960s and '70s. I never met my grandfather, her father. I saw pictures of him, and he only lived about an hour away, but we didn't know it and he died before I could get to meet him. I used to see my grandfather on my father's side, and he looked like he really didn't want anything to do with us, but then there were so many of us Witherspoon kids running around. I used to go and try to speak but he never really responded to me. My pop was a good guy; my mom might say a little different in private, but he was a good guy, and she never told me anything else. He wasn't good at giving us his time; he took me for rides in his car maybe ten times in my whole life. Despite all of this, I was happy. I had a father-figure in my life, even though my old man wasn't too interested in any of us kids. There was a guy around called Tommy Wade and you're going to like his story because he used to help all the kids and he was the biggest inspiration for me to get my career going. We'll come back to him later on. My father really didn't support me, even when I was boxing professionally. I know he wanted me to win and was always behind me, but I think he came to the gym maybe five or six times in all the years I was boxing.

Me and my brother Anthony started to go to the gym first, and our other brothers, Bernard and Stevie, followed us. Anthony had one hell of a punch; he's two years older than me and he was a light-heavyweight. He was also a very fast runner and could do the hundred yards in 10.2 seconds, and was a wide receiver for South Philly, All Philadelphia, and Pennsylvania all-stars. He went to a small college because his grades weren't so great, and they tried to get them better so he could go to a big university in Arizona State. Things didn't work out for Anthony. He had the scholarship but no money, and he grew tired of always calling our mom for help, so he came home. He started to take fights with people from California, and that's when he got a job in Pennsylvania Hospital where mom worked. I played tight end for Philly and I got a four-year scholarship at Lincoln University, in Missouri, but I was hurt really bad during a game by this big guy and I still get the pains in my back from that to this day. As a matter of fact, two the lower bones were bent downwards – you could see it in the x-ray they gave me – and these problems came back to haunt me later on as a boxer.

Anthony started out as a pro boxer with seven straight knockouts – five in the first round and the 56others in the second – and I used to hate to box him. He eventually went on to spar with Mike Tyson, and Tyson will tell you he gave him hard work. After that, I don't know what happened; he had a couple of defeats and he just died down, lost interest, and quit. He fought his last bout in England in 1990 against David Weir, but he was a real hard hitter who had 19 pro wins and seven losses in total.

All that stuff we used to see on the street corner – our uncles taking on those that were brave enough to have a go – it all sunk in, but it wasn't immediate; it took us time to come around to boxing ourselves. It's not that my uncles were fighting in gangs, and neither were we; all of us were just doing it for amusement and fitness. The boxing helped them to be known as tough guys, and it helped us to, but it wasn't the first sport I got into. The gang named after the street, the Emily Street Gang, used to hang out on the corner of Seventh and Emily, and my uncles used to be on the corner of Sixth and Winton. When I was a young kid, I didn't see that much of them but, as I got older, that changed. The truth is, I was around my mom's brothers, Jacob and Clarence, more than the Witherspoons but the boxing helped them to get a reputation as tough guys, and it helped us, too. I played football, baseball, basketball, bowling and golf at that age, and I even won a tennis tournament when I was 18.

I can't really tell you a lot more about my father; all I know was he was a jolly, happy, good guy. He's dead now. He was in and out of our lives and finally left when I was about nine or ten years old, but I don't think he missed a week's child maintenance after that and we saw him more than when he was living with us. He had three jobs. One was driving trucks and the other two were cleaning, so he worked hard for his money. After he left, I would go up to his place and see him sometimes and I'd steal money from his pants when he fell asleep on the couch and give it to my mom. She would yell at me and ask me why had I stolen from my father? She couldn't give it back because he would have beaten me for stealing. I saw him a lot when I got famous and he never asked me for money. I did purchase a shop – a store that sold hoagies and sandwiches – and he helped run it. I didn't really care about it at that time in my life because I was on drugs, and I eventually lost it. I only needed about $3,000 to save it from going bust. Every time I ran that store, I gave the food away, but I was doing a lot of crazy things during that period of my life which I will talk about later on. All I will say is that I wasn't any good as a shopkeeper because I'd make steak sandwiches for everybody; if somebody wanted one, I'd make it and wrap it up and give it away. People would come in late at night – friends and neighbors – and they'd try to buy their groceries, but I gave it to them for free. I didn't need to own a store; I just wanted to help people out. My father and my sister tried to run it like a proper business and I was a nightmare.

My earliest memory comes from when I was really young, about three or four; it was the day my mind really switched on to the world. There was nothing really special about what happened, and I think I remember it just because of the love I felt; I can still feel it now. All my Mom did was pick me up, and I can remember the smell of her clothes and perfume, and the feeling of just being safe. I also remember when me and my brother Stevie were playing with hot water. I had to be at least five or six. He poured all of this hot water over my stomach and we had to go and see a doctor. My mom carried me. It was dark and dangerous on the street at night, but she took me down the block, and she did that twice. They bust the blisters all over me. That's why I appreciate my mom – because she carried me around there, and I was a heavy boy. Stevie and I were being bad and I got hurt and I'm lucky I have no scars. My father wasn't around, so my mother had to look after me.

There was also an incident where Stevie was really ill and my father wouldn't take him to the hospital. I don't know why he wouldn't do it. Stevie was sick, rolling around in bad pain all the time, holding his stomach. My mom said "To hell with it", and she took him to the hospital. He was only 30 minutes away from his appendix busting and dying. He hated my father for that. He would talk nasty and I think he was resentful of him, and it all sparked from that one day. I guess he felt like dad didn't care about him. It changed his life because he almost died, and all my father had to do was take him to the hospital.

I used to be scared of Stevie. He was older than me and knew more than me; I wasn't a real tough guy when I was little. There was one guy called James Bryant who tried to pick a fight with my brother, and Stevie didn't want to go up against him. Then he said something to me and I just started swinging and it was over – I just iced him right out. Stevie was scared of this guy, who was tall and skinny, and when I beat the guy up is when it changed for me. I guess I grew in confidence. People have asked me whether that was the first moment I realized what power I had, and I can honestly say "No." I didn't even realize that when I was fighting. I never really got hurt because I had a good trainer who taught me basic defence. You see some of these old fighters today and they are all beaten up; you see them back in the day, when they were fighting, and their defence was poor and they were always getting hit in the head all the time; they're suffering for that now.

Another early memory was stealing milk from my sisters when they were in the crib and my mom saying "I know that baby didn't drink that milk bottle", and knew I'd had it and that I was hiding. I didn't know any better; the milk was good, and I can still taste it. I used to steal the babies' bottles and hide them and then my mom caught me and she spanked me. I was always the first one at the door waiting to go eat every day, too.

In total, there were eight of us. The oldest was my brother

Ralf; after that, there was Anthony, Stevie, and then me; next was the first girl, Cheryl; then Rosalind; my youngest brother Bernard; and, finally, my baby sister Fanny. My father also had two other kids outside of the marriage: Freddie, who we love very much, and Dionne. I used to see babies popping up all over the place, cribs and stuff all around. Everybody had big families and there were kids everywhere in those days. I remember my mom and dad telling me they were getting married; I was around six or seven years old at the time.

My education started at Francis Scott Key Elementary School when I was five years old. I remember my mom washing me up and getting me ready, before my brother Anthony and an Italian kid called Michael Ravello took me to school. After kindergarten, I went to school on Fifth and McKean Street when I was around eight years old. From there, I moved on to the Abigail Vare School on Moyamensing Avenue, the school in the Irish neighbourhood; Francis Scott was in an Italian area. Next, it was on to Furness Junior High, and then South Philly High, where I spent all my time playing sports. I was starting to see other kids' older brothers getting caught up in the gangs; there was drink and drugs about, too, and some of those guys started messing with it. Some of them started on the junk, some on the whisky. Then, later on, you started to see people your own age, people you grew up with and sat in class with, going the same way. Like a never-ending circle, it was a way of life and you were lucky if you didn't get caught up in at least some of it.

I remember one time there was this old drunk named Monkey Moe. I was only little, and we were shooting him with paperclips as he lay there drunk. He used to be drinking all the time and we used to torment him. One day, he almost caught me and I've still got the scars. I was messing with him, and then, when he chased me, I ran through the back alleyway. He carried on coming at me, so I carried on shooting at him with the paperclips. I ran and then jumped over a fence and made for the back door of our house which I always kept open in case I was being bad and had to make a dash for it, like then. My brother Bernard knew I was tormenting Monkey Moe, so he locked the back door to teach me a lesson. I crashed right through that door; I smashed my head, and I had a big gash. Monkey Moe never got me but I wasn't so quick to torment him after that. We were just like the kids from the Little Rascals movie; we used to make go-karts and race them down the street. But I never brought any trouble to my mom's door when I was little. I did when I was in fourth grade but, in the beginning, I was just a young kid trying to find out what was going on in the world.

With so many different types of people all living on top of each other, bad stuff happened. People needed their escapes from the harshness of life, and boxing was one of them. It was something you could watch on the television, or listen to on the radio, and I remember when Joe Frazier made his debut at the Convention Hall in Philly in 1965. He was the Heavyweight Champion of the World five years later and I remember thinking "Wow!" You sometimes saw him on the street, once he was famous. When he first moved out to Philly, he found work in a slaughterhouse and boxed in his spare time. That scene in the film Rocky, where Sylvester Stallone punches the sides of beef – that was what Joe did.

He used to go into the refrigerator room, where he would punch the beef. They used that in the film.

They say that childhood is the best time of your life, and I have some good memories thanks to my mom. She is something special; she had to be to have kept it all together like she did. She had to cope because she would have lost all of us kids, else. Sport was an escape for me and a lot of other kids on the block, not so much boxing in the beginning but the other sports I have mentioned, including football. When I was a kid and Tommy Wade used to be around, I played all of the time. I was going to be a footballer first before anything else, whilst people like Mike Tyson and Evander Holyfield lived and breathed boxing. They were always working out and sparring, and their fitness in the ring was fantastic. Mine was usually very good, but if I had felt the same way about boxing as those guys when I was a kid, and concentrated only on that, I think my fitness would have been much better. Unlike other kids, me and the rest of the guys Tommy used to help had something other than the gang. He was a highly religious man, and he used to make us go to church, too. He was a good man, and I would not have achieved what I did in my career if it wasn't for Tommy Wade.

Chapter Two

Mighty Crusaders

I SOMETIMES sit down and think about the past; I figure that's the kind of thing you do more of as you get older – all the years that have passed, and what is still left to come. You think about your children, life and death, God, and stuff like that. I also think back to all of the great times, some of which have passed into boxing history. I think of all the people I've met from so many walks of life – some turned out good, others turned out bad – but, when I was young, I could never have imagined the career I had. I think my biggest regret professionally was the fact that I did not take enough time to really work out some of the so-called friends and advisors I had around me. I think boxers nowadays are looked after a lot more; they have people trying to keep the wise guys out of their way, and that can work fine if the ones looking after the boxers are not on the take themselves; and what our group – the Raiders of Boxing – did has certainly helped fighters today.

There have been many stories in the news over the years, stuff about me and Don King, and other stuff that happened, too. I was really proud of some stuff: the birth of my kids; becoming the Heavyweight Champion of the World; other things too, and we'll get to all that later. There were also things I did, or got into, that I was not so proud of. Would I change all those bad things if I could? Of course I would, to some degree. Could I stop myself from having such a big heart? No way. What I am as a man, as I stand here today, all the good and bad, the power and glory, the awful stuff and the drugs…it made me what I am, and I'm not such a bad guy. Like I say, I did things I wasn't proud of, but most of my life, I kept the "Terrible" for the ring.

The Don King stuff left a bitter taste in my mouth; I learned the hard way. I haven't ever been the kind of person to wonder where every dollar I earned was going, but I wish I had kept a better track of things, maybe not trusted some people like I did. When you're making the kind of money I earned, you don't ever think it's going to end. Beneath the lights, stood in the middle of the ring, you feel like the most important person in the world; it was like a dream or a fairytale to me at times, especially when I was the champion. I guess you get so far removed from the realities of life, realities I would have had to face much sooner if it wasn't for boxing. I wonder where I would have been today without it? Probably living in the same neighborhood and doing my best to get by. I took my share of knocks, but it could have been a whole lot tougher without the fame and money. It could have been as hard as the times we had when we were kids. Those days, you really did have nothing. I've seen fathers getting stuff out of the dumpster just to feed their families; I have even seen people getting held up at knife-point, or gun-point, not because they are trying to steal a fistful of dollars, but because they were trying to get by with little or no money. That's why people turned to crime, ended up in jail, or got shot dead in some alleyway some place. I was fortunate that I didn't get dragged into all of that; I escaped, and I have people to thank for that.

I was happy when I was growing up. Tommy Wade would take all of us to the park when he was around, and I know he used to save his money up to help us. There were rumours he had over a million in the bank when he died, but you wouldn't have known any of that back then. He was special, but he looked like any other regular black man you saw on the street. He always used to follow me, my brothers, Butchie Knight, and Willy Perry. He came to every one of my fights: he flew to England to watch me fight Frank Bruno; he was there to support me in Vegas and all over the world. He groomed me and about six others to be football players, and we called ourselves "the Mighty Crusaders" because we were going to church then; we had Christianity. We would also play baseball, basketball, and football, but he never encouraged us to box, although he did have a pair of gloves we used to mess around with.

We would look forward to Tommy coming most weekends because he worked in New York City as a printer at NBC. He was also an actor who appeared in shows such as *Rawhide*, *Dragnet* and *Law & Order*, as well as writing shows for *Love, American Style*. The first was broadcast on CBS in 1969 and starred actors such as Henry Gibson and Ruth Buzzi. Tommy wrote two of them – *Love and the Fur Coat* was one of them. He was a very clever man and he had a heart as big as the ocean and really made a difference to a lot of people.

Tommy's main focus, though, was at the weekends when he used to come to Philly to make sure we played sports and were doing the right thing. All through the week, I wasn't looking for my father to come and make sure we were alright – I was waiting for the weekend and Tommy. When he came, we had to make sure we were doing well. He was a father to me, all my family, all the girls; every time he came to town, everyone was happy because Tommy was the nicest guy in the world.

There was never any fighting. Tommy was quiet and he was old; we didn't really know how old he was because he used to wear this hat to hide his baldness. In the end, it was sad because the wrong people got control of his affairs. He was in the hospital because he was sick, and I didn't know. I was with my daughter, Ayanna, and somebody told me that Tommy wanted to see me and that he was in the hospital. I said: "Wow! What is he doing?" I didn't know it was life-threatening, so I took Ayanna with me, and he looked really sick. I said: "Tommy, are you alright?" He was like: "Yeah", talking real low. He kept moving his head; he kept staring, and that was the look of death. He knew he was dying but he didn't want me to know. This was the man I loved – he was like my flesh and blood – and you could see the pain in his eyes. I said to myself "There's something wrong here" because I just didn't realize how sick he was until I walked into that hospital room. He called my daughter "Piranha" when we were teaching her how to eat and bite properly because she was so young. Every time we would go into the store when she was little, she would come out with candy that she had stole. She would bite right through the wrapper and I had to go back in and pay for it. Seeing him in that bed made me realize, maybe even more than my own pop dying, a lot of stuff about the nature of life and how fragile it is.

    I talked to Tommy for an hour or so in the hospital, and he said: "Tim, see if you can find a guy who can get me in shape when I get out of here." I told him "Okay", and to just get ready and to get well enough to leave. We were sitting there and he started falling asleep, and I called his name. He said "Yeah?" real quiet so then I got up and I said "We're going to go" and I gave him a hug and fixed his hat on his head, and his pillow, and I said: "Tom, we're going to come back." I didn't know he was that sick until I saw him but I did wonder if that would be the last time I saw him. Next time I went up there, when I was coming in, one of my Mighty Crusaders friends, Butchie Knight, was coming out with Tommy in a wheelchair and they were taking him to intensive care. They put him in the ambulance and that was the last time I saw him. Before all of this, Tommy told me we were going to write this book, record a documentary, and maybe make a movie. He was setting things up and we were talking all the time, looking at what I was going to do after boxing. He would call me and make sure I wasn't doing drugs and, before he passed away, he told a family friend called Jeanie Knight that he wanted to talk to me, but it wasn't until afterwards that she got the chance to tell my mother about his wishes. The fact that I missed seeing him one last time left me confused, angry, and hurt, and I still don't know what he wanted to speak to me about. He was sending me money to make sure I was okay, and I had been going up to New York and meeting with him a lot, making sure he was okay. I guess he figured out that his life was coming to an end so he wanted to get it all down in a book, or as a documentary, but it never came about. We were supposed to do other things and it just didn't happen in the end.

Tommy never liked to let anybody down so perhaps he wanted to see me to let me know that it wasn't going to happen. He was a shrewd guy; he saved his money all of his life, but it got into the wrong hands before he died. There was a family who lived down the street – the father's name was Apple; the mother's name was Julabell – they were nice people and I never had any problems with them. Their sons – Gregg, Craig, Baldy and Plug – were my friends; they worked in a shoe store and they were hard workers. They did a little hustling, too, to make some money but they were good kids and all close to Tommy. The first time I ever got high off of weed was in Greg and Plug's bedroom, but we were just boys messing around. I didn't want Tommy's money, but the way it disappeared...if there was anyone he would have left the money in trust for, it would have been our guys; it's what he would have wanted. Baldy, Plug, and Butchie Knight were like brothers to me; they took care of me because we were Crusaders. After Tommy died, I heard from Tommy's family that there was not much money left. In fact, he died before his mother (who we were close to, as well) and she lived until she was around 90. When she got old and frail, there were people who were supposed to be looking after her money, too. I knew them. Anyway, they were ripping her off. My mom was going down there and taking her to church and she was seeing all of these people going in and out of Mrs Wade's house so she started to realize something was going on. In the end, the police were called in. Tommy's mom eventually died and, at the funeral, my mom saw the person who was responsible for it all. He said to her: "Are you going to bust all of hell open?"

I was away in the UK at the time and she never told me and my brothers because she knew what we would have done. In the end, everything was cool and it turned out to be a misunderstanding.

My brother Anthony had 13 knockouts before things went downhill for him. He was going to be a professional football player – Tommy mentored him – and he went to Arizona State. His marks weren't good, so he had to settle for Tempe School in Arizona until he could get his marks together; he had to get ready. There were a couple of other guys Tom groomed to play baseball. You'd see him on the corner; he'd be with us, selling raffle-tickets, trying to make us money to go to baseball camp in the summer. It seems like he was always around. I remember him from when I was three or four years old and he knew us from when we were babies. He was just trying to keep us on the right track, not dealing with gangs, and we went to church every weekend. My mom made us go, but I remember doing my homework at Tommy's mom's house; my mom would make sure I had it done.

It was great to have someone around who promoted peace and harmony; it was also good to have something to focus on and think about, and I got pretty good at a few sports in the end. As I say, I was happy as a child. I don't know if any of us kids were 100 per cent settled, not having my father around that much, but I was still a happy. When my pop was around, there was sometimes harmony, or at least a ceasefire, between my parents, but I remember one time when my dad took some money from my mom and she was stood on the corner of Seventh and Winton with an axe. Here's a woman face-to-face with a big guy; she had an axe and she was ready to cut him. Everyone was out the doors, looking. I was little, and I saw it, and I said to my mom: "What you doing with that axe?" I was about seven years old. He gave her the money he had in his pockets and then he went some place. All she was trying to do was get us food, because we were starving. They say, if you deprive somebody of food for three meals, then they will turn to revolution. My mom had the axe because we had nothing to eat, our stomachs were rumbling, and my dad was out the door. I saw all of this whilst I was growing up; I knew what it was like to feel hungry, and my mom was forced to such measures.

My dad finally left towards the middle of the 1960s, when I was around eight or nine years old. In all honesty, there wasn't a lot of conflict between my parents but, when things went crazy, they went really insane, and super-quick. I didn't really see many big fights and arguments between my folks although I'm not saying it never happened. My dad was gone a lot when I was little. I'd see him, then he'd be gone for the next four days. I don't recall my parents showing any sort of affection to each other when I was little, but I do remember seeing them lying in the bed, laughing and joking. It was early in the morning; I walked up, but they didn't see me. They were talking and laughing, but that was it, that one time. I saw one big fight when we went to stay with my grandma; they called her "Gang-war Fanny". Later, I would call my grandma before every fight; I didn't feel comfortable unless I called her, and I used to do it right before I went to get ready. She would say to me: "Timmy, you know that hard rep you got; you better go out there and kick that boy's ass!" I didn't call my father before a fight– I called my grandma and I called my mom. My father died about five years ago; he was having dialysis – they stuck a needle in his arm and he had a heart-attack and they couldn't save him.

From the tenth to twelfth grade, I was at South Philly High School in an Italian neighborhood. I used to play football and baseball, also soccer from the ninth grade. I was the most valuable soccer player in Bernard Junior High. Recently, I have spent some time in England watching Plymouth Argyle, Sheffield Wednesday and some of the Premier League, where there is really big money being spent. In America, we don't have the fanaticism they have over in England for the game; the money is in football, basketball, and baseball, not so much soccer. When I was in junior high, I was tall, probably about 5ft 9in, maybe a little shorter. When I got to tenth grade, I was taller again and, by the time I got to twelfth grade and I graduated, I was 6ft 2in. Now I'm almost 6ft 4in and I don't expect to get any bigger. I grew all of those inches from the tenth to twelfth grade.

This was in the mid-1970s, when I was just finding my feet in the world. I was listening to the music of the Whispers, Bootsy's Rubber Band, and all those kinds of records. I was doing my best not to hang around on street corners and get into bad habits. In the news at the time was the famous *Rumble in the Jungle* fight which happened in Zaire, Africa. Muhammad Ali had been stripped of his title a couple of years before because he did not believe in the Vietnam War. He refused to be drafted to the Army and they suspended his boxing licence but, when I was finishing high school, this was over and done with. They couldn't keep Ali down, no way, but he did lose his first fight back against Joe Frazier, and then he got his jaw broke by Ken Norton. Joe went on to be the champion and Muhammad was going to retire. In the end, he carried on when maybe he shouldn't have done. He did beat Joe in the rematch, around the time I was graduating, and then there was all the spectacle of the *Rumble in the Jungle* and the *Thrilla in Manila* that was put together by Don King. Maybe Muhammad should have quit, but there is always that instinct in the boxer to come back for one more fight to try to recapture the glory years. I did it myself and, when my fitness was good, I was still capable. Like I said, my punching power was never in question, and many folks say even Mike Tyson could have been stopped by me if I hit him with my power. I love Mike – he's a great guy – but, with all the legal stuff I had going on with Don back at the time, and the agenda to make him the youngest Heavyweight Champion of the World, the fight between me and him never came.

As I say, my mom was really the backbone; she certainly kept things going. Her maiden name was Shirley Loman, she was born in St Matthews in South Carolina, and she's got a story of her own. Even now, I'm starting to find out all the different stuff about my mom that I didn't know had happened. She had a situation when she was growing up and her mom really didn't give her the right attention, and I guess that is one of the things that made her as strong as she is. When my father left, she didn't want to see us kids get split up and maybe end up in the situation she lived in when she was small. She's a strong woman who raised eight kids by herself, but I think her inner strength comes from her past. We may not have had anything when we were growing up, but my mother gave us all the love she had in her heart, and she did her best to make sure we came to no harm.

My first girlfriend was a girl called Linda Workman, but it

was like puppy love, I guess, when I was first in high school or junior high. It wasn't like real love, which you experience when you get older. Our lives were dominated by sports, which we started at a very young age. My uncle, Jake Loman, was another who showed an interest; he used to take us to sports – he took us to baseball all the time. Even after that time with my brother Stevie when I stepped up to the plate and iced James Bryant, I never thought of going into boxing, although I'd been in fights. Tommy Wade had taught us ball games primarily, nothing about boxing, and I never thought about becoming a professional boxer until I got out of university. I went to Lincoln University when I was 18 years oldand my best friend at the time, Keith Davis, who I'd been friends with since we were little, got us involved in a situation. We had a gang coming from Chicago to get us. My back got hurt in a football game and I told Keith I would not be able to help him. The kid who Keith had a beef with had a family that was were connected and they were coming to hurt us. I didn't have any real problem with this guy; to me, he was just some kind of wimp who couldn't do anything but say bad stuff, but I guess it got under Keith's skin, and that is how the situation developed. What I can tell you is that we made it out of the university just in time and went home; we were lucky. My mom never knew anything about it and she was surprised to see me back after only one semester.

When I joined the University, I had to pick all of these different subjects, and some of the teachers and coaches told me what the people in the physical education department looked out for. In other words, if I did certain things, I was going to get passed through. I didn't like that. I didn't even go to the classes sometimes and, when I went home to Philadelphia and they sent the marks through in the post, I was amazed because I still passed. I failed in other subjects, but I did pass physical ed because they wanted me to be in the football team. The reason why I became a boxer is because of my achievements in sports and the confidence it gave me, and I still felt like I had a chance to go on and become someone in the sports industry. Boxing was much easier because you didn't have to go to university. If you wanted to become a professional football player, you had to go to university for four years and get drafted to the team first; you didn't have to do any of that with boxing. All you had to do was go to a gym and train for a fight and, if you kept on winning, you could become a champion in five or six years. I would just walk into a gym, put the gloves on, and start training. I was lucky, but I guess I was also skilled. All these guys I was looking up to, the heroes of the ring and so forth, were around me. Here I was, just a kid, fighting out of Philly. Within a couple of years, though, I was lucky enough to turn professional and spar with the great man himself, Muhammad Ali.

Chapter Three

Mob-handed

I HAD friend called Eugene Milano who was in the football team with me. We were in the dressing-room in twelfth grade, and he was telling me he was connected, that he was doing stuff for the mob, but he was a very good footballer, too. He told me he was boxing and that was the first time I was ever asked to take part in it myself, although it was only a mess-around. As I already said, it was always around me when I was growing up, but I wasn't like one of these kids growing up who saw Joe Louis or Rocky Marciano and said to themselves: "That's who I want to be." I suppose I was guided towards football and other ball games because they were respectable, desirable at the colleges, and less dangerous than getting hit around the head for money. Even when I was thinking about getting in the ring, I was just looking at it as a bit of fun, maybe seeing it from a fitness perspective, not as a career move, at first. As far as I was concerned, I was going to be a footballer. Then something else happened at university. Everybody was outside the dorms, going a couple of rounds with this big black guy with bushy hair. They were calling him "Too Sweet", and he was beating everyone. On seeing me, he said: "Hey, how about a couple of rounds?" And I told him: "No." Then my friends convinced me, so I put on the gloves, and we went at it – boom, boom, boom! Then – bang! – I threw a right and it almost knocked him out; he staggered backwards, and he had to stop for about a minute. After about ten minutes, he shrugged it off and he started sparring with other guys once again. I didn't pay it any mind at the time; it did not register with me that I may have had some sort of a talent. But I did stop him.

Philadelphia has always been a boxing city, and there had been many world champions at all weights going back through the years, except for born-and-bred heavyweights; from bantamweight Danny Dougherty in 1900, up to heavyweights Sonny Liston, in the 1960s, and Joe Frazier in the 1970s, although those two weren't born in the city; they only came and settled later on. I don't know, maybe the atmosphere drew them in here like moths to a flame? Or perhaps there was the feeling that something great was going to go down in the city with all of its champions? Or maybe they could just smell the blood in the air? Do you remember that song by Bruce Springsteen *Streets of Philadelphia*? That just about sums up some of those neighbourhoods; you could just as soon get a gun in your face for doing something charitable out there on the street as you could get a "Thank you." My mom tried to teach all of us kids to be good people, although some of us did bad things along the way. We had some of Punchy in us; in our genes, maybe? I'm not saying it was all bad; not everywhere is like that and not all my childhood is awful memories – there's a lot of good in there. All I'm saying is that you had to watch your back all the time, and you could certainly find out really quickly that you were in the wrong type of neighborhood. Say you were an Italian who'd drunk a little too much and you wandered over into an Irish neighborhood and you started shouting your mouth off – you could find yourself beat up really bad, or worse. Despite all the terrible stuff, Philly had it going on when I was growing up, and has still got it going on today in the boxing world and in many other scenes, also.

When I was starting out as a pro, you also had people like world champion light-heavies Mike Rossman and Matthew Saad Muhammad (who died only a little while back), and bantamweight Jeff Chandler around you in the city; they were some of the local names who went on to win titles. To date, I am the only Philly heavyweight to win the world title, although we've got Bernard Hopkins who recently won the International Boxing Federation light-heavyweight title which is amazing because he was 48 years old at the time. Me and Bernard go back a long way. Sonny Liston was a Philly heavyweight champ, but he moved to Philly when he was in his mid20s, and Joe Frazier came to the city as a teenager in the early 1960s. Only Timmy Witherspoon went on to lift the world title, and his training ground was the streets of Philadelphia. When you see Sly Stallone in the Rocky movie, running through the Italian market, or at the Museum of Art in Philly, holding up his hands, that was me, that is what I did, and, like I already said, Smokin' Joe was the one who punched the sides of beef. We were doing all this stuff for real, and a lot of people used to wish me luck when they saw me out on the streets. I never really got into trouble with the bad guys, but I knew them because they played the sports that I played. Some even made it as pros, even though they were in gangs, and a lot of them tried to keep me out of trouble so I had a chance to make it. There were some influential people that used to cheer me on and make sure I didn't get hurt. A lot of neighborhoods fought in gangs, but mine didn't. There was a gang almost every three to five blocks and ours was small and we stuck together. I think people saw me as one of their own when I was a contender and later, when I was the champ. There were a lot of people who were pleased to see me; the last few years of the 1970s, which was when I started to get known around the city as an amateur and then as a professional boxer, was a good time for me.

Racism was still thriving when I was at college, and I remember being called a nigger and stuff like that. They wouldn't do it to me now because I escaped all of that. My mom taught me not to call a name back but I'm not going to lie – I called them a name back on most occasions, even when there was a big gang of white kids. I often got the better of a couple of them; sometimes, I beat up all the kids calling the names. Other times, I would not be so lucky, and I came home with busted eyes and split lips on a few occasions, but I was not a troublemaker; I tried to avoid it. As you get older, you understand some of the brutality you see around you a little better, and the boxing clubs took in some of the kids who were mixed up and from broken homes, just like they took in kids who were unwanted and angry, and they tried to channel that aggression into a positive force in the ring. That happened to a lot of kids, but not to me; you read the life-stories of a lot of my fellow boxers and they had those kinds of things happening to them. When the white kids called me names, I was prepared to fight them, but it was usually best to say stuff to them about their mothers – that was a way to hurt them back more than them using the N-word. I would still get into trouble if my mom caught me using swear words; I was brought up never to cuss or be a racist. I suppose she tried to stop us from thinking that way despite some of the things I have seen and heard when I was growing up.

At one point, when I was little, we had a white family living with us. My mom took in a sick lady who was her friend, called Miss Effie, who later had to stay a month in the hospital. So my mom took care of all three of her young children in our family home; us kids slept in our room in cribs. They were white kids; she was a Greek lady who had fallen on hard times when her husband left, and then she got sick. My mom raised us kids and her kids for about a month-and-a-half in total, when she didn't need to. She believed in what the Bible says about helping your fellow man. But when Miss Effie got well and got everything together again, she turned her back on her and we never heard anything from her again. Mom was real upset. You would think that would be enough to stop her from doing charitable things like that ever again, but not my mom. I used to see Miss Effie on the street, and she couldn't look me in the eye, so she had to live with that in her heart. Some people don't have a caring bone in their body except for when it suits their purpose. My mom never taught us to be that way; she would always talk to us about what was going on around us in our surroundings.

I also remember around this time that there was an English lady who came over to our school as a volunteer and, as soon as I saw her, I was in love; it was my first childhood crush. Her name was Pauline and I was only five years old, but I was besotted with her. She came over for the summer camp, and she would come to our block. She was so beautiful. I'd never seen anyone like that before in the flesh, or heard someone talk in that English way. She had blonde hair and, when she passed by, people couldn't help looking at her. When the summer ended and she left, I was heartbroken. I often wonder where she is now, whether she is still alive and whether it would be possible to find her. She would be pretty old now.

It's funny how time just gets away from you. It seems to speed up, the older you get, and it's crazy to think that all this happened about 50 years ago. All the characters from those days, the great times and memories I have, seem so fresh in my mind but, in reality, many of the friends and teachers I had around me are now long dead. You never think of things like that when you're a kid. You don't think about death; it's all about that false sense of confidence and getting to places real quick so you can get on to the next thing. Dying is something in the movies and in soap operas that you don't take much notice of. There is no real significance to it all until you become older and nearer to it, and maybe that's good. It isn't natural for people, especially kids, to spend their time thinking about such things because life is for living, after all. But you never forget those that have gone.

I eventually thought to myself that maybe I should try boxing. I knew I could do it. Like I say, I'd seen my uncles fighting, and I didn't want to be like them. I'd had incidents on the street and in the playground, and I'd sparred a little with no gloves against Too Sweet and Eugene Milano even though, when Eugene first asked me, I said "No" because he was kind of muscled and big. Years later, when I got into boxing, I found out he was one of the main guys who testified against the mafia, but he was also one of the guys who first got me into boxing. He is infamous for breaking the mafia's code of silence in return for a reduced jail sentence, and I have to admit he was just one of a couple of sportsmen around me who got caught up in all of that stuff. When I came home from university, I was sitting around with my brother Anthony and we heard a couple of our friends were boxing, and then everybody seemed to be doing it. Buster Drayton was another one of our guys; he started boxing at light-middleweight and he turned pro in 1978. He won the vacant International Boxing Federation middleweight title in 1986, which was a good year for us Philly boys. There were a couple of other guys who were boxing too; my brother Anthony had his 13 knockouts, and there was a guy called Kenny Reese who was a middleweight from South Philly, although he didn't have his first pro fight until 1983.

    We decided we would go to the gym and give it a try because I felt my life couldn't just be how it was at that point in time. I knew I wasn't born to just work in Pennsylvania Hospital, which was what I was doing. I was living down the street from my grandmother and just working, and I needed something else, a bigger challenge, because I was a sportsman. I was late into boxing, and I think that did put me at a disadvantage over some of these guys who started out as little kids and spent their whole life growing and training specifically for boxing, not for football like I did. You speak to Mike Tyson and Evander Holyfield – they lived and breathed it all their lives. I was working in the kitchen at the hospital, and I had this burning ambition but no idea which way to go. Then this old white guy came into the line in the canteen where we served the food, and he said to me: "You're Tim Witherspoon, I heard about you playing football; you're too young to give it up, what are you doing?" You've got to get into something." That's what triggered my brain.

With those words in my mind, it somehow made it much easier for me to go to the gym. Time was moving on if I was going to make it in sport, but, like I say, I still wasn't really thinking seriously about boxing. It would have been around the mid-1970s when I got my wake-up call. I just felt confident that I could do well at all kinds of sports and I wasn't afraid of getting hurt. I'm not saying I was never nervous before I entered the ring; I'm a human being, after all. I'm just saying I wasn't afraid of taking a punch, or giving one. I did not see myself as being special, or being different from most other average boxers. Becoming a pro-footballer, or basketball player, would have been a lot higher up my list than becoming a boxer. I was probably heading for the wrong side of the tracks if people had not got involved with me. They helped me to become better than some bum hanging out on street corners all my days, drinking. What that old guy said to me in the canteen made me start to question everything, but I knew I needed to work hard if I was going to be somebody. Like I say, I just felt like I had it in me. I don't know why I felt like that, but I was just confident in myself and my abilities, and boxing gave me the focus and the determination I needed to succeed.

So there I was, working in the hospital and training in the evenings. In the hospital, we would set up all the tables for when the top surgeons flew in from all over the world. I also did all the domestic duties in the kitchen, and that was about the size of it. I remember my mom and dad coming home from watching a Gypsy Joe Harris fight at the Philadelphia Arena one night, and there were lots of other boxing occasions. I sometimes wonder what else I could have achieved as a professional if I had trained as a boxer from an early age. I figure I still did pretty well, though. Once Anthony and I had decided we were going to give it a go, we went to the old Passyunk Gym in South Philly, which was in an Italian neighborhood, and we had to walk in and walk out every day. There was this guy, a numbers writer, "Old Man Bishop", they called him, and he knew all the boxing people in the city. He also knew all the mob guys and he kept saying to me and my brother that he was going to take us up to the gym, but we ended up going up without him and we started training with the wrong guy, although we didn't know it at the time. His name was Clarence Booker, and he did a lot of stuff with me, my brother, Buster Drayton, and some other guys, but it wasn't necessarily the right stuff he was teaching us. I was coming away winning fights, but I was getting hurt. I was getting punched in the face too much; I was getting busted up lips and taking too much punishment. My quality was beginning to shine through, but he was teaching me the wrong stuff.

The Passyunk was a famous gym in Philadelphia, alongside Joe Frazier's Gym. A lot of fighters in South Philly trained at the Passyunk and Juniper Gyms. World champs Matthew Saad Muhammad and "Joltin'" Jeff Chandler, who are both from South Philly, trained there, as did many others. In America, as soon as you start training, you are considered an amateur there and then and you're going to get an amateur fight. You don't just go into a gym to train; when you first walk in, you know they are going to get you fights. Right from the beginning, everybody was saying I was showing potential and soon the guys at the other gyms were saying "Wow, I wish we could have got them Witherspoon brothers" because they knew we were training with the wrong guy. Buster first took us in there with Clarence because he was training with him and, when we bumped into Old Man Bishop, he told us we had gone to the wrong guy; he wanted to take us to see someone else. I said to him that we were training and that we weren't going to leave Clarence, so we continued. There was also a southpaw called Randy Mack, who was a veteran, and, after a few months, they put me in the ring with him and I did well. They were looking at me and my brother from the first day we came into that gym because they knew we were going to do pretty well, so we kept on with it. I was still working in the hospital until, one day, a surgeon called Ira Schwartz came along with his father and he told me they had heard that we were boxing and showing a lot of potential. He asked me if I knew a guy called Slim, and I told him I did. Ira said that he could help us to progress. That is how I got introduced to Slim Jim Robinson.

Chapter Four

Doctor Snow

THE Schwartzes took us to meet with a Jewish guy named Mark Stewart who was a part of the hierarchy at WMOT (We Men of Talent) Records in city. They were the guys responsible for making soul records in the traditional Philadelphian sound and they had a couple of big sellers, too. There was one in the early 1980s by a guy called Frankie Smith, who wrote music for the O'Jays; his single went to number one in the Billboard chart sand sold over two million copies. Anyway, Philly hospital is on Eighth and Spruce, and we had to go to Twelfth and Spruce to meet him. We walked into the office and he was there with his associates and they told us what we could do, and everything they could do for us. I said "Okay, that's great, let's get it started", and that's what we did. I was still working at the hospital at the time but they were going to help Anthony and me get into this thing. We were both happy that people with a reputation and money had faith in us, and they obviously had the contacts. The record label itself only lasted about ten years; they finished up in 1984, when there was a whole host of lawsuits about money laundering and stuff like that. During the time they were active, they were serving up "hits" in and out of the studio, as it turns out. They liked us even though we had no idea what we were walking into.

Slim Jim Robinson was a clever trainer and, like many of the great boxing teachers, he was a good boxer himself back in the day. He was tall and skinny and fought at both middleweight and at light-heavy, and he was one of Sonny Liston's main sparring partners, so he had a really good education. Slim was an amateur champion who had 15 knockouts and he was from south Philly, like me, born there in 1930. It was Slim who convinced Mark Stewart that we could go all the way in boxing. He said that, if we listened and trained well, then we were all going to be alright. What made it better is we were gradually getting to the point where they said I didn't have to work in the hospital any more. They gave me and my brother an apartment and a car. Well, they gave it to me first, I should say. My brother Anthony wasn't sure on the deal at first, and he signed a month later and we started living at Wellington House on Twelfth and Spruce. Mark and Slim knew we were training with Clarence Booker and we weren't happy. Larry Holmes was the Heavyweight Champion of the World at the time and he heard about me and wanted me to be his sparring partner; he was going to pay me $800-1,000 a week and they contacted Booker, who never told me. When I heard about it, I never confronted him – I just left. Matthew Saad Muhammad was going up to the mountains, to Deer Lake, Muhammad Ali's training camp, and I started up there with him. That's when I realized that my trainer wasn't good enough to take me all the way. When I was up there fighting with Saad and his guys, I was winning fights, but I was leaving with bloody lips and bruises on my face and that's when it really dawned on me that Clarence wasn't the right guy. Trainers try to keep you from learning about who the good trainers are so they can have you for themselves. They know they can't take you all the way and I found that out the hard way.

The Juniper Gym is only about a quarter of a mile away from the old Passyunk. Both are Italian places, in Italian areas, and, after I left Clarence Booker, I started going to the Juniper every day. After that, I went up to Muhammad Ali's training camp where the great man himself saw me training with Saad Muhammad; I was his main sparring partner by then. Ali was hanging out with everybody and talking, and everybody would stop training to watch him. He was coming back out of retirement and, when he saw me, he said: "I want you to be one of my sparring partners." That was another step on the ladder for me. Ali stayed up at Deer Lake for about a day and a half and I guess he liked what he saw in me. I was in awe of him, really, and we were following him around, asking all sorts of questions; he was real generous with the time that he had. Saad was staying at Ali's cabin, and I stayed in another with his trainer Nick Belfiore, who tried to get me to sign with him. Later on, when I was sparring with Ali, I also stayed there. Saad was training to fight the English guy John Conteh. I think this was around the same time they were starting to think about putting together Ali's fight against Larry Holmes in 1980.

One of the guys who put me on the ladder to start with was from WMOT; his name was Larry Lavin. He seemed to be just a regular guy, a dentist who was living quite a lavish lifestyle in the suburbs of Philly. It turned out he wasn't so regular after all; he was one of the main cocaine dealers in the city and he was reported to be making five million dollars a week – you may know him better by his alias, "Doctor Snow". When I met him, I didn't know anything about what was going on – he didn't get busted until the mid-1980s – and all I saw was people sniffing all the time and thinking they all had colds. I was kind of naive to it all, I guess. Larry said he had bought into the label and that he was making all of his money from record sales, which of course turned out to be untrue. He ended up getting a long prison sentence for all of his involvement and it came as quite a shock when I found out the truth. When the net started to close in on them, they tried to sell me to Don King, but, to be honest, I didn't want to go. In the end, the feds came and busted them but it was only because they got too greedy. That song by Frankie Smith I was talking about earlier, the one that sold two million copies, was called Double Dutch Bus and when they didn't give Frankie his royalties, he couldn't pay his taxes; that's how the FBI came into the whole thing. They were running such a watertight secret business, there wasn't anybody outside that inner circle that knew what was going on. At the end of the day, Larry was backing us financially, giving money to Mark Stewart, and we didn't even know where the money was coming from.

Before I turned professional with Mark, I had seven or eight amateur fights for Clarence Booker. I lost my very first fight and when I look back on it, you can see that something was wrong with my trainer. He put me in the ring with a guy who was a five-time Golden Gloves champion and I got beat.

My mouth was bloody, I was bruised, and I said to myself: "Man, the rest of my career can't be like this fight." You never put a guy who's just starting out with a Golden Gloves winner, although he never stopped me; I lost by a split decision. I remember that I won my second fight against a guy called Titch. There were two guys with the same name, one was a big giant from Pennsylvania, and the other was from New Jersey and I beat him twice. I dropped him in the first – boom! I was jumping up and down thinking that the fight was going to end and this big guy just got up off the canvas and then he hit me and hurt me. I came right back fighting, and I dropped him in every round after that.

My last amateur fight was against Joe Frazier's son, Marvis, for the Golden Gloves, and I lost. That's when I really started to think my trainer was the wrong guy, in a way, and it was coming into my mind that I was going to leave. When I heard Old Man Booker turned down the offer from Larry Holmes, that made up my mind; I was really angry. When I got into the fight with Marvis, I was coughing and sneezing and my mom insisted I shouldn't be fighting because I was not well. So, I'm in the dressing-room getting my hands wrapped, and my trainer is saying to me "Don't cough, don't sneeze" and I'm thinking to myself "There's something wrong with that", telling me not to cough. Have you ever tried to keep it in when you're busting to cough? He shouldn't have let me fight; I was weak. So we get into the fight and I shot my load in the first round and hurt Marvis. Then he won every round and, at the end when I came out of the ring, the first person who came up to me was my mom. I said to her "I tried" and she told me I should never have fought that fight. I just did it because it was time to fight; a better trainer would not have let me get into all of that.

Deer Lake is about ten miles from Pottsville, Pennsylvania, and a lot of people from the town came up to the lake to watch. Many came up there to try to capitalize, to try to make money and sell stuff. There was a guy called Aaron Snowell, who used to come to the camp and watch me and light-heavyweight Eddie Mustafa work out. He also saw Ali's corner guy Bundini Brown, who was cool with him. I never knew Aaron, who used to be up there with his family, drinking beer, and Slim said to me: "Tim, what's this guy hanging around here for? If he's going to hang around, he's going to have to get up there and run with you; he's going to have to train with you, or he can't be around. You have got to start really training. We don't want no beer or stuff like that. We've got to shake things up." I said to Slim: "Alright." Then I spoke to Aaron and I said: "Look, man, you're going to have to start working out.", but Slim had already told him the day before. He was cool with that, and from there he went as far as being in Tyson's corner although he had never ever fought before. That's how he got into the boxing game; he started running with me, chopping wood and training, and, from there, Slim started teaching him how to train people and he ended up in my corner, Slim Robinson made him my second.

I used to love fighting at the Blue Horizon in Philadelphia. I had my last amateur fight against Marvis Frazier there, and it's where all the greats of Philadelphia appeared. It was an historical place that closed down a couple years back, which is a shame because The Ring magazine once voted it the number one venue in the world. The atmosphere was always amazing and, because it only held about 1,500 people; it kind of had that intimate feel to it. If you were from Philly, you aspired to fight at the Blue Horizon; it was like the Mecca of local boxing. I was still working in the hospital, doing the dishes, when I fought Marvis and a lot of people came and watched me and they waved spoons in the air. They were chanting "Spoon! Spoon! Spoon!" I know it doesn't sound too good now, but that what they were shouting; it was only later that I got the nickname "Terrible Tim". After I lost that fight, I went home and I was embarrassed. I wouldn't go outside. The next day, I'm sat in the house and I'm thinking to myself "Why am I embarrassed? I'm going to go outside" so I ran down to the corner and everybody was saying: "Good fight, well done." They were just happy that I had fought and I was in there with Joe Frazier's son, because I was from their neighbourhood. I thought it was going to be negative, but it was positive. People were patting me on the back and saying "Good try" and I didn't expect that.

This was the time it all started to come together with the doctors, and I was introduced to Mark. Anthony and I were going back and forth between the hospital and the Juniper Gym, where I first started sparring with Saad Mohammed. I was also at the Passyunk but, like I say, I cut away from there and Clarence Booker. It was Slim who really put the icing on the cake with Mark Stewart; he really had faith in us and that is how we turned professional. Now, I didn't know how Slim knew Mark Stewart and I'm not sure how much he knew about what was going on with the cocaine business, to be honest. As well as a trainer, Slim was a very clever detective and bounty hunter – he would go and get criminals and lock them up; he wasn't scared of stuff like that. He was allowed to carry a gun and it may well have been that Mark and Slim had conversations in private about what was going on but, like I say, I never heard any of it. I would see Slim at the gym because he was training Mike Rossman, who was the light-heavyweight world champion at the time, and they told us about the doctors who were interested in backing us, but Slim never said he'd be training me. It all snowballed from there, really; I can't tell you when we got on a salary but it wasn't long until I quit the hospital.

To sign a professional contract, both parties have to be licensed in the state of Pennsylvania. What we did was just trust our new managers. Although it took Anthony a little longer, they were being recommended by good people and we signed. They promised us things and they didn't rip us off; they gave us a good deal, I remember that. Along with the apartment and the car, they gave me $250 a week – it later went to $500 – and I was happy; I was doing what I wanted to do and now we were going to have the proper people around us to help us grow. I was excited. I'd spent so much of my time washing dishes and just existing after I knew I wasn't going to make it in football; I wasn't sure where my life was heading, even though I had the boxing and I had my family around me. There was a lot of talent about at the time, but also there were people out there looking and trying to find up-and-coming fighters and I did enough with Old Man Booker to get noticed. I regret not listening to people now but if I had taken a different route, I could have been in there quicker. Once I was pro, I got a shot at the world title within four years, but I think I could have been ready a lot earlier if I had figured it out about my trainer a little sooner. It felt like a weight had been lifted. We were doing okay and things were looking up for us. I started to see Larry Lavin around the offices of WMOT quite a lot. He would come in and talk business with Mark Stewart, but

I never overheard anything or suspected anything at all. There were singers and other media people around there at that time, also boxers and newspaper people. It was a professional organization they had set up and it was hard to believe when I found out what they were really doing.

1979 was a good year for me, and it was a good year for boxing, although things didn't work out too great for Mike Rossman, who was stopped by Victor Galindez, and he had to hand over the World Boxing Association light-heavyweight belt. Larry Holmes won back his World Boxing Council title against Mike Weaver, but, boy, did Mike give him a hard time. Of course, 1980 saw Larry beat Muhammad Ali at Caesars Palace but, without taking anything away from Larry, Ali was way past his best. He was 38 years old at the time and Larry didn't want to fight him because he knew it would be a blood-bath, but Muhammad needed the money. It was around this time that Ali developed a bit of a stutter and trembling hands. Going into the Larry Holmes fight, he was on medication, too. He got beat up real bad and his trainer stopped it in the 11th round. People were pleading with him to retire but he had one more fight against Trevor Berbick in 1981, and he lost in the tenth to a split decision. Many people say these last two fights really contributed to the Parkinson's Syndrome he later developed, and it was a real shame to see such a legendary figure reduced to fighting on just for the money. Ali's advisor Jeremiah Shabazz told me that, after the Ernie Shavers fight in 1977, Ali said to him "Look at my hands." They were shaking, and that was the beginning of his illness. I know a lot of fighters do fight on – I did it myself – and it isn't just for the money. Of course this is a huge contributing factor, especially if you have had bad advisors, or deals have gone sour. You become accustomed to a certain standard and way of living, that whole cycle of recuperation after a fight which leads you then to starting to think about the next opponent. After a while, you're back building up your training and focusing; your whole life is governed by that fight for months on end. When the big day finally comes, you are so pumped, there is such a buzz going through the media, and, of course, the people at the event; you kind of feed off of that and become accustomed to it. You never think about it being taken away when you are a contender, or you become the champion. I didn't really make plans for after boxing, although I knew my career couldn't last forever. There was nobody showing me where to invest my money and keep it safe, and everybody wanted a piece of me at the time. Like I say, boxers today are more protected; back then, we were pretty much on our own, or we had people taking advantage of us. We are fighters, few of us are businessmen. I wouldn't say I was bitter about it because life is too short, but there are a lot of guys who suffered, a lot of fighters who got ripped off and had to go through a lot of trouble, before somebody sat up, took notice, and started to change things for the better.

When I was with Slim, he never gave me any indication that he knew what was going on and, like I say, I would see him talking with Larry Lavin and Mark Stewart, but he wasn't afraid, and he wouldn't hesitate to take chances or gamble. Slim and I got really close and tight because I understood that he knew how to train me correctly and that was my only concern. I didn't really know what training was about until he took me under his wing. Then I started venturing off, not leaving him, but seeing other trainers all over the city. These other guys were teaching me new things that really benefited me as a boxer. After a while I was thinking "Wow, I've got a good trainer" because he was teaching me how to block. I knew it was good stuff. I'd also tell him personal stuff because my mood was a big part of my training, my feelings contributed to how I conditioned my mind. It was like I had to put myself in the right frame of mind before I got up on stage and performed. Getting into the zone, the place I needed to be in my mind in order to fight my best fight, was really important before I threw my first punch in the ring. If I was having a bad day, Slim would pick up on that or I would tell him. He was like a big brother to me, but you couldn't tell him everything. He was clever. He was like a father, brother, and trainer all rolled into one until he started working for Don King. After the feds busted Larry and Mark, we ended up with Don but I don't think he respected Slim. Don knew he was a good trainer but he could never get him fully on board because Slim was loyal to Mark Stewart and that's the way it was. I saw Don recently and we had a hug and I told him I loved him. He can be a great guy and all of the things that happened between me and him happened a long time ago. None of this disguises the fact that we haven't always seen eye to eye and it's a shame we couldn't have figured something out back then, rather than dragging it all through the papers and almost ending up in court. But that's the way it goes sometimes, I guess.

Chapter Five

The Pros and the Cons

WHEN I first started fighting professionally, I was with Linda Workman, who is my oldest daughter Linette's mom; she was my high-school sweetheart. I didn't have a father around to talk to me about women and what you should do when you get a girl, so I was a little naive, but I think it was a big thing to just be with just one girl when you are young. I really didn't have leaders around me telling me the best way to go at the time, so I just trusted my instinct. My father wasn't there to say "Hey Tim, there's a nice girl, why don't you settle down with her?" and I think I needed that influence. Don't get me wrong, there were several people I had to answer to if I did something wrong but that was all I had to put me back on track, and a child needs a strong father-figure.

Linda was the kind of woman that any man would want because she was gorgeous and really, really sweet and nice. She treated people with respect, even though she could be bolshie, but that's only because she wanted me to do the right thing. She didn't want me to scream and shout because of the neighbors next door, I remember that. She didn't swear; she didn't cuss; she went to church; and, after a while, I started to think that she was too good for me. I wasn't a bad guy but I had an idea of what the boxing was going to get like. I was going to be away a lot of the time, travelling; it was going to be too much for her to handle. She was there supporting me for my first three or four fights and then things started to go sour. She came to the gym with me a few times, but this just wasn't her world. She was bolshie in the right kind of way, but there was no way I could have done everything she needed me to do, and the career I was carving out for myself was the final straw, so to speak. I do have some regrets about that, and I think, if all of the pieces could have fitted in nicely together, we could have had a really good life together. She would have helped me to manage my money better and not be deceived the way I have been in the past.

I started going in a particular direction with my life and Linda wanted to go in a different direction. Naturally, she wanted to make a nest with our daughter, and it isn't like I didn't want to settle down at some point, but everything was moving really fast. With each fight, I was getting stronger and wiser during those early days as a pro, but I couldn't see a way of balancing everything I was doing with the kind of family life she wanted to have. I was out there, meeting new people. I don't mean women and stuff; I mean I was making the kind of contacts which would take me places and I guess maybe I saw getting married as being anchored. I wasn't exactly scared of it and, looking back at it now, I really think I made the wrong decision; maybe I could have achieved that balance. She was my perfect lady, my childhood sweetheart, and if only I could have seen a way to make it work, we could have been okay. Out of bad comes good, of course, and obviously I wouldn't have had my other kids if things had worked out with us. When you're young, you've got all of those hormones running around in your body; so many roads you could go down; so many challenges leaping up in front of you. I was starting to feel kind of important and building confidence in myself for the first time in my life, and maybe if I had been brought up in a "homely" kind of way, with a mom and a dad, with routine and stability, maybe I would have made the decisions I made back then from a more secure perspective. If you don't have that, I think it can lead you on to make more off-the-cuff decisions and, if I am being honest with myself, I think this was certainly the case with me sometimes.

When Linette was born, I was down at the prison fighting this guy who was an inmate. His name was James Scott and he got a lot of exposure for that. We were sparring and the Press came in – it was quite a story because he was one of the most dangerous prisoners on the east coast. The prison was called Rahway and they had the boxer Rubin Carter in there. He was jailed for a triple homicide which was later overturned. His story is remembered in the 1999 film *The Hurricane*, starring Denzil Washington, and the Bob Dylan song *Hurricane*. James Scott had three or four fights on NBC and CBS Sports, and they went into the prison and filmed them. He was a genuine contender for the World Heavyweight Championship until the WBA decided to remove him from their ranks towards the end of 1979. They figured having a man who was in prison for robbery was not a good for their image, and ABC Sports decided against televising his bouts for the same reason.

I went into Rahway with Slim. We had to go through three or four locked doors, then we had to get an okay from the governor to go in and train with Scott. As we were leaving, he made a bet with me. He bet me $1,000 that I couldn't knock him down. Slim said: "Let's take the bet." I'm boxing him in this massive gymnasium filled with inmates; I think they had around 300 people in the place to see the fight. Slim says to me: "All you need to do is get inside and put your left foot around his ankle and push him down." When we made the bet, he didn't say how to knock him down, he just said "Knock me down" so that's what I did. You've got to remember that this guy is a mean guy, and nobody messed with him. So, I pulled his foot and knocked him down, and when he hit the ground, everything in the gym stopped, you could hear a pin drop. Then, he gets up and he's going crazy, but Slim was a player. He was real intelligent and he says to him: "You didn't say how we were to do it; you just said to knock you down." Which is exactly what I did, although but he didn't pay me the grand.

After sparring with James Scott, I got the call to say that my daughter had been born so I went down to Pennsylvania Hospital and I saw her; she was in an incubator. She was so beautiful. I guess it was all there, waiting for me, but the boxing was gradually taking hold and it started to get impossible to fit it all in. After that, I started travelling more, which put a strain on the relationship and we started to get a little distant. As time passed, getting married got to be a bigger thing for Linda and it kind of snowballed, but I still thought it was the wrong time and she would pressure me about it. It's crazy because she was the girl I wanted to get married to, but this was just the wrong time for me. We had the baby, and my career was taking off big-time, and people were telling me I could be the Heavyweight Champion of the World and I wanted to prove them right. The businessmen backing me had invested a lot of time and money in me and it wasn't like I could have just thrown it all away. In the end, I think what we both wanted, what would make us happy, was too far apart from one another. When we came together as I family, we were not happy, and no kid should be brought up in a home where the parents feel that way; I'd seen it myself as a kid.

After hanging out at Deer Lake, it all started to come together for me at the start of the 1980s. The camp was outstanding, the facilities were fantastic, and it was good to just get out of the city. I think I first started sparring with Ali at the end of 1979 into 1980 as he was getting ready to fight Larry Holmes. In the end, I became friends with him and he would come to my fights, and he sparred with me for my fight with Tony Tubbs. He was in Georgia and he came down especially to help me out. When I look back at it now, I regard myself as lucky because I had a real good boxing education; I learned from some of the greats and some of the guys who had worked with the greatest boxers of all time. You get so lost in the preparation for a fight that maybe you don't take that extra minute or two to really appreciate that fact when it's happening. We leave that for much later in life, when you reminisce at it all and say "Wow!" It's not just the good; I also remember the bad times, too. Like I said, I never went out of my way to hurt anybody, and I certainly didn't set out to do anything wrong. Life doesn't always pan out as you want it to, though.

Why didn't I get married to Linda at that time? Sometimes I regret it but, like I say, I had so much other stuff going on.

None of my other brothers had been married and I didn't want to be the first, so that was another reason. It sounds stupid, but that is the way I felt about it back then. My mind was focused on my boxing and Slim asked for six months to get me in shape for my first fight and that is when we really started to work hard. I was doing most of my work at Deer Lake, then I came down from the mountains for my first pro fight against Joey Adams, before going back up there afterwards to prepare for the next. There was a whole bunch of guys fighting out of Philly. There was me and Anthony; there was Frankie and Anthony Fletcher; there was Marty and James Shuler; and the Howards. There were four brother teams fighting in Philly at one time and sometimes we'd be on the same bill. I first appeared on the same card as my brother professionally on June 17, 1981, at the Martin Luther King Arena in Philly. I beat Bobby Jordan and Anthony knocked out a fighter called Brian Morrison in the first round; it was his first pro fight.

What I remember of my first professional fight against Joey Adams was that it was at the 69th Street Upper Darby Theatre; they had all these different fights up there. It was the walkout bout (the last fight of the night) and the waiting was like being on Death Row. I was sitting in the front row all night watching the other guys and I had to wait until the end. Later on, when I was sat in the dressing-room, and then when I started to walk out, I felt really good and the crowd got behind me. I could see Mark Stewart and a few of his guys all there behind me 100 per cent, too. I was a little nervous but it went really well and I ended the fight early. Joey was really strong but I was taking no prisoners; the bell rang and I would say I knocked him out within a minute.

Like I've said, in the beginning, I didn't know what I had because I wasn't old enough and I didn't have enough experience; all I knew was that I was in shape and Adams was 60lb heavier than me, so I did good. I had the company behind me and I didn't want to let anybody down. I can still recall what Slim taught me in the gym. I remember because it's like going to school; you never forget those times. When I first went in and trained with Clarence Booker, Slim was in the gym and he first looked at me then. All these other trainers were looking at me with their mouths watering, thinking to themselves: "Why is he training with Old Man Booker?" So, I was training right next to Slim Jim Robinson every day in the very beginning and he saw something in me, and he knew my trainer didn't know anything.

What was it about Slim? Before a fight, he got you ready mentally. He was a good defensive boxer, very clever and slick, and he taught me all about that. He showed me how to throw punches, and how to avoid taking them, and, of course, he's the one who taught me how to throw my famous overhand right. The stuff that I was doing gave me more confidence; I just felt like a better fighter straight away. The difference between Booker and Slim was like night and day. I started picking up and learning so fast; it was incredible. I fought Larry Holmes for the world title in 1983 and I had only started out with Slim four years earlier. I had gone from undeveloped, virtually unknown, to having a crack at the world title. You've got a lot of good boxers out there that go ten, maybe 15 or more, years before they get a shot at it. I had a handful of amateur fights, then 15 pro-fights, and I was given a chance. Tommy Wade had given me a good grounding; he taught me how to be professional in my affairs and not to be confrontational. I had to be good at sports, else Tommy wouldn't be happy; that's the way I thought about it then and that competitiveness just stuck with me throughout my career.

In the beginning, I wasn't even eating right – I was eating pasta and stuff like that. As I started travelling and meeting different people in the gym, I began to educate myself but it wasn't like today where they monitor everything that goes into your body and build you up so you peak as you get into the fight. I only really started to eat properly when I met a guy called Percy Custas who was a sparring partner for Saad Muhammad, too, and we used to go around together. They called for him because he was from Philly and, when he arrived at the camp, he started me eating a lot of fruit and really showed me how to eat right. We are still friends today. I still see him. How we used to work it was he would get in there and spar with Saad Muhammad, then we would swap and I'd get in and finish it up. Nowadays, he's got his own gym called Shulers and we sometimes train there.

When I was with Clarence Booker, he also had Buster Drayton who went onto be IBF light-middleweight champion. I grew up with him; we were from the same neighbourhood. There was also Earl Hargrove, who knocked out his first 24 opponents, and there was Kenny Reece. We were all from Philly and we all kind of learned and trained together. We would mess around and I'd say to one of them "I bet you I'm going to get a knockout." We were betting each other all the time when we were fighting as amateurs. Each one of us would be trying to get the knockout first. I guess we were kind of confident. Each fight I had, I learned something different from – how to prepare for my fight and eat properly, for example – because I didn't know anything. After one fight, I learned how to move better; after another, I learned about calisthenics. I also learned how to do defence better. I was learning from everybody around me. I never used to lift weights but I wish I did; I did a lot of running and, when we were in the woods, I found chopping wood was very beneficial. I wish I had known about sports medicine like these young guys are doing today; that didn't come in until a little while later.

One time up at Ali's camp, this guy turned up from LA and he had all these different gadgets and they were experimenting on Ali. I was saying: "Hey man, why are they driving him crazy?" They had him wired up; they were monitoring everything like he was some kind of guinea pig. I didn't realize what he was doing was the stuff I needed to be doing. This was the new science and technology coming into the sport and I wish I'd been involved with all of that right from the start. We were watching them drill him, and having him do all these different power-steps and all this new stuff that boxing wasn't doing at the time and I didn't realize it was the sort of stuff I should have been doing. At times during my career, I struggled with my fitness, and I think it is a lot easier today to keep in check, and to peak just at the right time. They can do a lot of stuff and really keep an eye on a boxer and make sure he isn't doing damage to himself. Can you imagine how much better some of the greats from the old days would have been if they had all of today's technology available to them back in the 1930s and '40s? People like Joe Louis, Rocky Marciano, even Ali, would have benefited because Ali's golden years were during the 1960s and early '70s when none of that was going on. I also wonder how many of the old fights would have happened because of something the machines picked up. I heard about boxers like Ed Sanders, who tragically died in the ring. Before the fatal fight against Willie James in 1954, he was complaining of shoulder cramps and headaches, and today it wouldn't have taken place; maybe he wouldn't have died. I saw a lot of boxers get messed up by taking too many punches to the head, a lot of good guys, and I was as sure as hell that I wasn't going to be one of them. Slim taught me how to defend myself properly.

Chapter Six

On the Road

THE second fight I was offered was against a guy called Robert Ritchie but I was nervous because it was going to take place in Lynchburg, Virginia. If the name of the place doesn't give away why I was a little edgy, all you got to do is look back at its history and you will see that it has a strong association with the Ku Klux Klan, and I wasn't sure what kind of greeting I'd get. Since the 1960s, the Klan's numbers and activities have died down considerably but the south was unknown territory for me and I wasn't sure they would be cool with a black guy fighting in their city. We drove into the town and checked into the motel and, as soon as I was in my room, I automatically closed all the windows and doors and locked the place down. I'd seen and heard all this racist stuff before back home, and I imagined things were a whole lot worse here, but there was no burning crucifix out there on the lawn and everything was kind of still and quiet.

I was getting ready to fight Ritchie but I was more concerned about getting attacked and stuff. Once we'd checked in and got ourselves together, we met a couple of people and talked to them, and then, when we went to the mall and I saw black and white together, that made me feel a whole lot more comfortable. I went to the store and I saw a white guy laughing and joking with a black guy, and that really put my mind at ease. I weighed in, and then we went to the fight and I won by a knockout in the first round. I was so happy. I just took him right out, I think it was within 30 seconds or one minute, and people in the crowd were amazed with how easily I had beaten him. I guess this was the first time they had heard of Tim Witherspoon.

I remember that my third fight was up at the Long Island Arena in New York in May 1980. The town is called Commack. It's only a small place, but it was another new experience, and by now I was starting to get into the swing of things. I was in good shape and I was only 23 years old; people were starting to really take notice of me, although I wasn't making the big headlines just yet. I fought a local guy called Robert Evans who was also new to the professional game, having started out in 1979, like me. He had lost his first fight, drawn another, and won three (one by knockout) and I knew I could beat him although it was real hard work.

I don't think I was cocky and expecting a knockout in the first again, and I have to say he gave me one of my toughest fights in the early part of my career. I was hitting him with a lot of punches, but he was aggressive and I had to dig deep and keep in check if I wasn't going to get hurt myself. I managed to win every round and then I knocked him down in the sixth and won by a unanimous decision. When I dropped him, I thought that was it, but he came back at me really aggressively. I guess I could sense the fact that he was hurt a little and I just continued to throw punches until it felt like my arms were going to fall off. He lasted the whole round before the judges made their decision but, afterwards, I knew I had been in a fight, although I was getting a lot sharper and better at my defence. I wasn't coming away with busted eyes and split lips like I did when I was with Old Man Booker.

By the summer of 1980, my baby girl Linette was growing away really nicely, but I think both Linda and I knew things were not as they should be. If I had been a stay-at-home kind of guy with a nine-to-five job, I think we would have been okay, but I can't honestly say that would have been the way forward for me; even if I had taken a regular job, there were no guarantees. I loved Linda but I guess that just wasn't enough. I'm not saying she wasn't there to support me; I've already mentioned that she did. There was so much going on around me at the time that I don't think I really had the chance to be sad about the situation for too long and when I got to see Linette, I could do it in my own time, at my own pace, without the pressures of having to be a husband as well. That is how I felt at that time. I'm not saying it was right but I had to try and fulfil the potential people saw in me, and I didn't want to let them down.

In 1980, things started to change at WMOT Records, too. They merged with another label and they expanded their offices in Philly and LA, as well as signing a pressing and distribution deal with CBS. After this, they released Frankie Smith's *Double Dutch Bus*, which was certified as a gold record, and Barbara Mason and Major Harris also had big hits around this time. There was a heatwave in America that summer which killed a lot of people and it made training and sparring even harder as I was busy getting ready for my next fight. We sometimes went up to Deer Lake and, other times, we were in Philly, but I was fit and strong and looking forward to what was to come. My fight against Robert Ritchie made me realize that I had to work even harder as the fighters were just going to get better and better, although I hadn't been in the ring with any chumps up to then, that was for sure; every one of those guys I fought early on had the ability to beat me. Even though I didn't really realize the ability I had, I knew, if I kept on winning, I had a chance to go all the way like people were saying I could. I had the confidence of youth, you might say.

My next fight took place in McAfee in New Jersey in July 1980, and Linda brought Linette up there to see me. I was up against a fighter called Charles Cox, from Boston, and he was a little bit shorter than me, but the fight wasn't easy. He came at me –he was much heavier than me –and he was no pushover. The fight took place at the Great Gorge Playboy Club which had been built by Hugh Heffner in the early 1970s. It was a great place and I managed to knock Cox out in the fifth round which took me just a little bit further up that ladder to where I wanted to be. I had a great support network around me at that point with my manager Mark Stewart, and things were going great. I was earning some good money, too – I was getting around $20,000 a fight – and it wasn't just me, remember; my brother Anthony was looking really good, quick and powerful, and he was getting ready for his first pro fight the following year. We were happy. Nobody was trying to rip us off, and we were being looked after. It's just a pity things didn't stay that way. I ended up losing some of the best years of my professional career in the end and you can't help but wonder what else

I may have achieved if I had been able to stay with my management team.

    The relationship I had with Mark Stewart gave me a lot of security and stability, and later on, when it all went down with him and he went to jail, things started to go wrong for me, too. He had big plans for Anthony and me and we were going to go to the top together. I think we would have, too. Our plan was bigger than Mike Tyson's and Cus D'Amato's. Mark took care of us, but it wasn't going to last forever. I can still remember him giving us the guarantee that Don King would give us everything we deserved when he eventually tried to sell us to him, and when he said that, I was comfortable with it. Mark convinced Larry Lavin to purchase the Arena in Philadelphia, where they used to have professional roller-skating, and he decided to hold fights there. Anthony and I were in a good situation; we stayed in an apartment in the office building where the record label was, and there was a good vibe around the place. They also had other boxers around like Bernard Hopkins and his uncle Art McCloud; there was also the middleweight Sterling Quick. I knew the singers Brandy Wells, Fat Larry's Band and Captain Sky, and my daughter Indya's mom lived in the building, although I didn't know that until later, when we got together. We interacted with most people there, and this was a really positive time for me so I felt really good about taking my first fight in my home town.

    The Philadelphia Arena was really run down when Larry bought it, but it was known for holding boxing contests in the past. They re-named it the Martin Luther King Arena, and called the basketball team the Kings as a gesture of goodwill, and they fixed the place up. It was a really good venue, with all sorts of teams playing there, and I have so many memories. Later on, when Larry stopped giving money to Mark Stewart, the good times ended. In the end the place got burned down, but by then the FBI and the Internal Revenue Service were already looking into these guys. My first fight there was against a Jamaican guy called Oliver Wright, who was ten years older than me, and he'd had 30 fights. He'd been in the ring with Larry Holmes and Ernie Shavers, although both men had beaten him, so I just went for it. At the end of the first round, the referee had to escort him back to the corner, that's how many body shots I was hitting this guy with. He could have stopped it, but he didn't, so I just went at him again in the second round. I knocked him down three times and the fight was over.

So everything was booming and I was moving too fast. This was a new decade and these were exciting times, until it all came crashing down. Thanksgiving came and went in Philly. They have the Gimbels Parade there, which is a big thing, and I remember watching it as a kid. I started to think about the next fight. I was trying to focus my mind because there were so many other things to think about and I had to be that narrow-minded. Linda was living in South Philly with my daughter and I was taking care of them even though we were living apart. She was so nice to people and her ways rubbed off on me. I wasn't a bad guy but she had this way about her – she was gentle and kind – and I didn't want to come across as different. I have so much to thank her for and it is tragic what happened to her in the end; it still cuts me up now, the way she died so young, but we shall come back to that later on.

James Reed was another tough opponent who I fought

at the Martin Luther Arena on December 11, 1980. I remember, at the time, there was a worldwide outpouring of grief coming out of every radio and TV set because John Lennon had been shot dead a couple days before in New York City. The radio stations were playing his music over and over, and the TV stations were going crazy because a lot of people loved the guy. Reed had been a sparring partner to some of the top contenders. I think he sparred with boxers like Gerry Cooney, who fought Larry Holmes for the WBC title a couple years after me and lost. I put pressure on him all fight and I managed to knock him out in the sixth round. I was around 195lb at the time and I was in good shape. In my first 14 months as a boxer, I'd won my first six fights and stopped every one of my opponents within six rounds, so I guess six was my lucky number. Also, if you take a look at my shorts, you would always see the words 'Raiders of Boxing', which was our gang that went against wrong-doing in boxing; I was keeping it going, which would be vital later on when everything went down with Don King.

Next up, was Ed Bednarik, from Pittsburgh, in January 1981. We were both undefeated at the time so I was thinking people thought this one had a chance of going the distance. I was working as hard as I could and chopping a lot of wood up at Deer Lake. Like me, Ed had been a pro for just over 12 months; he'd fought four times, and he'd KO'd three of his opponents; and all of his fights had been in Virginia. So I guess I had the home advantage, if you like. I always believed in my trainer and he said to me "Tim, no problem - you're going to knock him out" and I did, in the first round. I guess Ed was expecting someone a little less than me but I hit him with a right and the show was over for him and that's when everything started building up for me. For whatever reason,

Ed called it a day after that fight against me. All I know is that I hurt him and this fight opened doors for me.

My next opponent was a guy called Marvin Stinson, who was also from Philadelphia, and he had been an amateur champion. I had met him before, and I think I may have sparred with him, too. He was an older pro; he was intelligent; and he'd never been beaten. He'd fought 15 fights, won 12, and drawn three, but he'd gone the distance a lot of times, so I realized he was tough. I knew him, and he knew me; he was also a sparring partner for Larry Holmes. Marvin knew a lot of stuff and he had experience; I didn't have any experience at all, but I had guts and willpower; I was young and up and coming and I didn't want anybody to beat me.

That fight was my first ten-rounder, and I just had to win it. Marvin tried some tactics in the beginning, pushing me when the referee was reading out the information at the start. He tried to do stuff to intimidate, just like Larry Holmes did. Then he pushed me again and I almost fell and I told him "I'm going to knock you out" and I almost did. I almost had him in the first round, but then his experience came in and I realized I had to just suck it up and be strong and do what my trainer had taught me, and I won the decision. It was one of my big wins early on because we were both from Philly and we were both undefeated. I feel kind of guilty because his next fight was going to be for big money and I stopped all of that, but I had to do what I had to do.

I realized that Marvin was the first sparring partner Larry Holmes' people had sent, and he was going try and keep throwing them at me. I still see Marvin today and he is a good friend of mine. After our fight, he had a couple more that he lost before he called it a day. I slowly started to realize that Larry's camp at least had their eye on me and this kind of made me sit up and take notice. As I say, my life was full of positives – everyone was pushing for me to succeed and Tommy Wade was still around and he was delighted for me. I also had Muhammad Ali coming to some of my fights now he had finished boxing himself, and when I look back on it, I have to say that his presence gave me a huge boost, and it was a great honour. Ali's last fight, dubbed Drama in Bahama, was in December 1981, and it took place a month before his 40th birthday. It was against Trevor Berbick, who won by a unanimous decision after ten rounds, but, by then, Ali was a shadow of his former self.

    I fought Dave Johnston at the Concord Hotel at Kiameshi Lake, New York, and I knocked him out in the fourth, which set me up for a fight against Bobby Jordan in June 1981. By now, everybody knew I was up and coming; they were starting to hear the name "Witherspoon"; and I was knocking people out along the way. With Bobby, the referee had to escort him to the corner because I hit him with everything that I had. There were fights where I had to be a little bit intelligent or just soak up the pressure and I didn't like to over think things too much, but in other fights, I was like a wild animal fighting for its life and that's how it was with Bobby. I just wanted to get in there and box. I remember that I hit him in the corner and he kind of froze and the referee grabbed him by the hand. I thought it was over there and then but they finally stopped it in the next round after a knockout. It was a good fight; Bobby wasn't as difficult as some of the people I'd fought, but he was certainly game.

By now, everybody was coming to beat me so I knew I was doing something good. Larry Holmes was holding the WBC heavyweight title at the time after beating Ken Norton In a hard fight at Caesars Palace in 1978, and he had defended it 12 times by the end of 1981. He not only beat Ali, but also Trevor Berbick, Renaldo Snipes and Leon Spinks. However, he knew that I was on my way. By the time we met in May 1983, Larry had a record of 42 fights, 42 wins, and 29 knockouts over a ten-year period. By 1983, I'd been a professional boxer for five years, but already I had become a top contender. By then, I'd won all 15 of my pro fights, and recorded 11 knockouts, so a fight against Larry was always going to be regarded by me as the fight of all fights, but his guys threw a couple more at me first, though, just to see if I could stand the heat. I was strong and confident and I was starting to think by now that maybe my chance of a shot at the title was going to become a reality after all.

Chapter Seven

Rising Up

THE second fighter Larry Holmes' camp threw at me was a guy called Jerry Williams, from North Carolina, and he was really strong. I think he was Larry's number one sparring partner at that time, and the fight took place at the Martin Luther Arena in Philly; it was my fifth fight there, and it happened in July 1981. I was starting to feel comfortable with the venue; it was my home arena and everyone I knew was turning up and supporting me, including my family and my uncles. No longer were they shouting "Spoon! Spoon! Spoon!" because "Terrible Tim" had arrived and it was a great time to be alive. It wasn't about the publicity or the pay days I was starting to get – I just felt so proud and honoured to be rising up through the ranks, and to be earning money doing something I enjoyed. Despite everything I had been taught by Tommy Wade and all those other guys, I'd still found myself cleaning dishes and doing menial stuff for a living. If it wasn't for that old man in that dinner queue that day, I wonder where would I have ended up?

It wasn't just about having the talent, or the mental and physical ability to box. It was also about being in the right place at the right time, and, like I already said, I was fortunate to have so many champions and great trainers and managers around me at the time. I wanted to be like Ali and Saad Muhammad; call it the confidence of youth, but I really believed I could do it. It was like my religion, and I just had to keep the blinkers on and stay on the road if I was going to get to where I wanted to be. I wasn't just on the take – I had the ability to help some of my friends and family as I made more money, and I did that. I was fit and healthy and ready to face whatever was coming at me. I'm not saying I was never nervous. When you've got a huge crowd out there and you're on television, when you've got people like Muhammad Ali sat in the crowd watching you, sparring with you, and telling you you're going to do it, there is a certain amount of expectation to go out there and win.

I remember that Jerry William just kept coming at me like an express train, and I kept hitting him and I was glad I'd trained as hard as I had, believe me. This fight was the second step towards fighting Larry Holmes myself, but I didn't realize it at the time. Larry was starting to think to himself "Hey, this guy Witherspoon - it could be a hard fight if we got it together" so I guess I was getting closer to going up against the champion. I beat Jerry Williams by TKO in the seventh, and he had never fought anyone with as much power as me before. Winning that fight set me up for three in a row in Atlantic City. The first was against a guy called Curtis Gaskins, who I knocked out in the second, and I'd probably say that my opponents coming up were tougher than Mike Tyson's when he was proving himself as a champion.

Next, I was lined up for a big fight against Alfonzo Ratliff on NBC TV, which was the first time I had fought in front of the cameras. Again, you get a little nervous when you think about all of those people out there, watching. Fortunately, I was able to focus myself, and once I'd traded the first punches, I forgot all about that and just got on with it. Alfonzo was big and undefeated, and he went on to win the WBC cruiserweight title in 1985 when he beat a guy called Carlos De Leon. A year later, he fought Tyson in Vegas and he was beaten. In the first round, I could hear someone in the crowd shouting "Terrible Tim" over and over and I came out of the starting blocks good and strong. My memory is that we both hit each other hard for six rounds, and then, in the seventh, the deputy commissioner, a guy called Percy Richardson, voiced his concerns over my breathing. I was doing okay, but he kept putting his fingers in my mouth and I was wondering why. He was trying to help me breathe, but I was okay. I was tired and I was getting hit, but I was on top and before they could react, I turned up the heat on Alfonzo. I finished him off against the ropes. We were in the middle of the ring and he was trying to hit me in the stomach and I was kind of pushing him away. He was trying to grab me but I moved forward and I hit him with seven or eight shots to the body and the head and his legs just gave way. He fell into the ropes and the referee called it off. I was so happy that I had got such a big result and I can remember looking down at all my people – my mom and my grandma; Tommy was there, too. They were looking up at me with tears in their eyes because they knew, deep in their hearts, that they were the ones who had put me in that ring with all those years of teaching and nurturing. They were the ones who helped me to grow strong and gave me a hand-up to being where I was.

I was around the same weight as Alfonzo, who was from Chicago and who boxed really well. I was the first man to beat him. After the fight, I realized I was at a crossroads for the first time. This was it, the first time I heard Don King in the audience - it was him shouting out my name, and he wanted to sign me up. He just kept yelling "Terrible Tim, it's only me and you" and when I looked down, I didn't really know what was going on. I said "What's up Don?" and I spoke to him for a little while. The fight was a technical fight and we were picking at each other all the way through, figuring out where we could hurt each other. People saw it in America and in different parts of the world, and suddenly I had arrived; in the mind of the public, I was truly a contender.

The fight against Alfonzo was a great fight for television and we became good friends afterwards, training in Don's camp, running in the morning and working out, and the fight was one of the biggest in my career in terms of me growing. Afterwards, I had so much more confidence than I did when I first started and my mind became a different place. I was becoming famous but I have to say it didn't really faze me. People talk about hangers-on in boxing, because of Ali and a lot of other stars who had these kinds of people around them, but the majority of people who were around me cared about me. There are lots of people out there who would love to get money and be a part of something big, but I didn't look at it like that. I had a lot of friends I didn't know come on board, I must admit, but I wouldn't say any of them were close. I had friends from the neighborhood that assisted me. There was a guy called Taleak Eddie Burgess who gave me the name "Terrible Tim" although somebody put it about that Ali did it. It wasn't him; it was Taleak, who was a guy I grew up with. One time when I was working out Ali said to me "You're terrible", meaning I was devastating in the ring, but it was Eddie who first gave the name to me.

I wasn't really thinking about the championship; I was thinking "Maybe one day I'll be there", but that was it. I was living day by day, inch by inch, and just listening and learning. My brother Anthony was fighting, too, but I wasn't really thinking about how many millions I could be making. My next fight was scheduled for March 1982 and, by the end of that year, my brother had fought six times and had six knockouts, so we were quite a team. He fought at heavyweight, light-heavyweight, and welterweight, and nobody had lasted more than two rounds with him at that point; he was one hell of a puncher. He did the same against Randy Coleman in March 1983, stopping him in the first, before he lost his first fight in June. It was against Charles Williams in Rhode Island and it was a points decision, but I think he was unlucky.

The fame and the money was great, of course – it was fun – but I was just old Tim. It didn't make me better than anybody else; I was just the same guy. So was my brother. The thing is, I didn't know how to organize money, and I didn't know how to be a business person. In my mind, I wasn't thinking about buying property, or investing, and stuff like that, and I wish I did know more about it and had kept my money closer to me. I think I've always been a little too trusting, but I can't help that because it's in my nature. I want to believe somebody is good and truthful but, like they say, in reality, you can count those people on one hand. They tell you they are well-meaning but, at the end of the day, they are just out for themselves. Early on, I was protected from that; whilst Mark Stewart was around me and Anthony, we didn't have to worry about any of that stuff. And, of course, there were the Schwartzes, and I don't think I would have met Mark if it wasn't for them.

I did go to university and played football but, when I was a professional boxer, all I was thinking about was fighting, training, and going to the gym. I didn't think about becoming a multi-millionaire to buy beautiful cars and houses. As a matter of fact, with the money that I had, I never bought a brand new car in my whole career, so I wasn't really materialistic. People could walk up to me and I'd say "Hi" and be their friend, and it wasn't until later on down the line that I learned that you had to play a certain role because people could take advantage of you.

I've said that my father wasn't around to keep guys away from me, and, of course, when I lost Mark Stewart, it was just me and my brother against the world. Maybe if my father had been around me all of the time, things would have turned out differently. I'm not shirking responsibility for the bad decisions I have made in my life; I hold my hands up to all of that. What I am saying is I just wish I had learned, I wish I had been taught about all those important things in life like money, women, and, of course, people, and how devious and sneaky they can be: guys who pretend to your face they are your friend, then they go stab you in the back. Tommy taught me about sports, discipline, and a little bit about religion, but I still didn't get the influence of my dad rubbing off on me like boys should get and I don't think a lot of those bad guys would have been around me if I had. I was streetwise and I had commonsense, but having the right influence from your parents, from your father, is a lot better than hearing it from some place else.

People had heard of me before I was on TV because I had sparred with people like Ali, Saad Muhammad, Gerry Cooney and Trevor Berbick, and word got around that I was up and coming. It was around this time I figured something fishy might be going on between my promoter and Don King, and they hooked me up with a fight against this guy from South America and told me he was the champion down there. His name was Luis Acosta; he was from Argentina and he had won the Latin-American heavyweight title in 1980. The fight took place at the Playboy Club in Atlantic City, and we were staying there and training – me, Bernard Hopkins, Arty McCloud, and my brother. We had a little deal with them down there in Atlantic City; we were going down and training and fighting and it was really good.

The fight against Acosta lasted two rounds. I hit him with a right– it wasn't an overhand, it was a straight right –and I hit him with a couple of body shots and he went down. He came at me a little bit but, when I did that, it was over. It was then that I noticed that the following I had was getting bigger and I think it's because people knew I was a good person. They knew I had respect and I wasn't really a hothead who nobody could get along with; I was easy-going, and I didn't like negativity. Mark Stewart was a very clever businessman and he told me he was going to negotiate and make Don King pay me the money I deserved if we signed. Mark was very charismatic, very-sharp, a good talker and a good looking businessman, and I was really hurt when it all went down; it definitely set me back. I loved Mark; we were good friends. Every day he was saying "What do you need?"

and he was the kind of manager any up-and-comer would have loved to have had.

Renaldo Snipes was one hell of a fighter. He was born in Houston in 1956, so he was 25 years old when we met. Like me, he was undefeated right up until he met Larry Holmes 11 months before we got it on in November 1981, and he also gave Larry one hell of a fight. By the seventh round, Larry had become frustrated and thought he would have had an easier time against Renaldo, but it just hadn't happened. Renaldo had been cut, but he'd looked good, going so far as knocking Larry down in the seventh, so I knew I wasn't in for an easy ride. He hit him with a right and it took Larry out and everybody though they were in for a surprise, but Larry recovered and he went on to beat Renaldo. I still believed nobody could stop me, and being around all of these champions was making me stronger every day. They were pushing me and trying to steer me in the right direction.

At my fight against Renaldo in June 1982, he was a little bit ahead of me in terms of experience – he'd had 24 fights and I'd had 14 – but it was that fight that made me realize I was then fighting for Don King, because he promoted it. I was in the training camp and I came home seven days before the fight and I messed around with a lady. I also had a couple of cans of beer and a little bit of sex, and I felt kind of weak in the knees and a little bit nervous before that fight; I think you can tell, if you watch it. I was more aggressive in the opening rounds, but once Renaldo got his jab working, it was starting to cause me a few problems, and he hit me in the nose in the second and I was bleeding a little bit. I was trying to get in there, but he was boxing quite patiently and waiting for an opening, and he was getting in some good hooks and crosses. By the fourth, there was some swelling around my right eye and we were really going at each other. When I came out for the fifth, I knew I had to try something a little bit different and when he got inside, I grabbed hold of him rather than letting him do damage. I also connected with some good crosses and started to get on top again. He was coming at me hard, but I kept my composure and just threw it right back at him, and a grazing jab actually cut him in the seventh round. It then became a war of attrition for the next couple of rounds as we chipped away at each other without really looking for that knockout punch. I think we were both tiring and maybe saving something in the tank for the end, but I still felt I was on top and he didn't want to risk making that cut any worse. By the 11th round, I thought I had him; he looked very tired and I just kept working away, thinking maybe I could finish him off, until the last round, when he caught me with an uppercut. I managed to get some good punches in, opening up his eye even more and it looked as if the referee was going to jump in, but he didn't and the bell went and it was over. I had won again, this time at Caesars Palace in Vegas, and I had my own battle wounds to show for my efforts.

I'm not taking anything away from Renaldo but I was not as sharp for the fight as I had been previously. I could tell because, when I was up at the training camp, I was feeling tired, and you know your own body and your limitations. I was really tired towards the last rounds, more tired than I usually was, but I got the decision because he was running from me and wouldn't fight me. He was moving around too much, so I just kept on getting my shots in and doing this and that. He just didn't do enough to win and I did, simple as that.

After that fight, I was on top of the world. I was the number one contender and I'd beaten both of Larry Holmes' sparring partners, and now I was looking at Larry for what he had done to Muhammad Ali. When Renaldo had knocked Larry down, he looked really tired and vulnerable, but that was the thing about Larry – just when you thought he was finished, he would come back big and strong. Against Renaldo, in the sixth or seventh, you see Larry against the ropes for 30-40 seconds and you think it is all over for him before he pulls something new out of the armoury. With a lot of boxers, when you see them fade like that, it makes you want to finish them off – you're smelling the scent of blood, so to speak – but Larry was different. Larry lulled you into a false sense of security and then – wham! – you were on the floor, counting stars. This never happened to me, of course, but during his 21-fight defence of the title, he KO'd a lot of guys, and now it was my turn to get into the ring with the champion of the world.

Chapter Eight

Looking at Larry

MIKE Tyson once said he beat up Larry Holmes because Larry had defeated Muhammad Ali – this is how much respect all us boxers have for Ali. Really, I was the one who first gave Larry a whooping for Ali, but they gave the fight to Larry because people had a long-term plan for him. After Ali quit boxing, things weren't right with him, and he was diagnosed with Parkinson's disease in the early 1980s, when he started to show tremors in his hands and his speech was slurred. I know that, after his fight with Ernie Shavers, he was really sick, and knew something wasn't right when I was sparring with him and he was telling me off because I would not hit him in the body really hard. It is possible that boxing had nothing to do with Ali's condition – sometimes people can get a viral infection which leads on to Parkinson's – but, come the end of his career, the doctors were prescribing him drugs to stop the tremors. I think he really was the greatest of all time, but he carried on way too long, when he should have been financially secure.

Why do I say it was me that got Larry back for beating Ali? I say that because I won our fight in May 1983. Watch it on the internet – I show no fear and I'm strong all the way through. Ali's old trainer Angelo Dundee, who was commentating that night, said I had won it, like most others who were ringside that night, as well as the crowd, who were with me all the way. When it was over, I stuck my hands in the air, I was raised on shoulders, and you see Larry despondent in the corner. I was there when Larry fought Ali, and I can remember the doctors telling him he shouldn't fight. I sparred with Larry for that fight, and he returned the compliment and sparred with me before I fought Tony Tubbs and Frank Bruno in the UK. On the way to my shot at the title, I had beaten all of Larry's sparring partners, and I was the first guy to really beat up on him, but I will give him credit for staying on his feet in the ninth round. I have to admit I was a little pissed about the tactics he used before the fight and, of course, the outcome, but everybody that matters in my life know that I won that fight, and so does Larry Holmes.

I remember when Don King told me he would get me the fight, Slim was saying he felt it was a little bit too fast for me. In the end he said: "Tim, believe me, you're going to whip his ass." So I did. When we were leading up to it, I was training hard and chopping a lot of wood, and I was getting the best boxers to spar with. I had broken my jaw a year before; one of my stable-mates, Lightning Bob Smith, did it – he was a great heavyweight. We were training and it just happened. So, it had been 11 months since my last fight against Renaldo, and Larry had fought and beat Randall Cobb and Lucien Rodriguez in that time, and both those guys had taken him 12 rounds. When he stepped into the ring, he had already defended the title 14 times after beating Ken Norton in 1978. For about four or five months, I could do nothing, and then I got the wires out of my jaw and they offered me the Holmes fight. I said "Yes", and there was a lot of stuff leading up to that fight.

Larry was saying a lot of negative things about me, that I was a bum and that I didn't have any money. He was telling the Press he was going to knock me out and that I was nothing. I come from a city where we don't take stuff like that. Whilst Larry was getting ready for the fight, I was building up a lot of anger – who was this guy to say Tim Witherspoon is nothing? He sent a lot of spies to see what I was doing, and what shape I was in, so I knew he was worried about me because I had beaten his best fighters. I hadn't seen it before. Building up to the night, there was a lot of fighting going on between his brothers and my brothers. He was trying to put my family down, saying that we had nothing, saying the only thing we had was the desire to win the Heavyweight Championship of the World, and he was dead right about that; we didn't have anything. I still didn't fully know the ability I had, but I was starting to believe that I could win it.

About 18 months after I fought Larry Holmes, Larry Lavin was getting out of his car and a police SWAT team pounced on him and he was greeted by a federal agent with a pump-action shot gun in his hand. This all came about after Frankie "Double Dutch" Smith had made his complaint to the IRS because he wasn't getting the royalties from his record. Next thing you know, me and Anthony were getting evicted because the building was going up for sale and everyone was going to jail. That's when we got sold to

Don King, and that's when both our careers started to go downhill – and I know that sounds crazy because I became the Heavyweight Champion of the World under Don.

From having people behind us who were going to make us rich and famous, we found that we had to try and re-establish ourselves under Don and, of course, we weren't businessmen; mentally and physically, we had to go in another direction. It is funny how things can change so quickly in life sometimes: in May 1983, I was fighting for the Heavyweight Championship of the World; and then, at the end of the next year, everything was falling down around my ears. One thing about us Witherspoon boys is that we are tough – we don't take any shit from anybody – and, in the end, I got a settlement out of court from Don, but it cost me some good years in the ring. I believe he put me in some really bad situations but, after all this time, I don't bear any malice towards him. I've said before that I saw him a couple of years back at a show, and we had some pictures taken together for the media; he told me that he loved me, and I told him the same thing. He's an old guy now, so I guess he's getting closer to his day of judgement when his creator will be weighing up whether he's going to be going up or down for eternity, and there will be no way for him to influence the outcome.

I was training in Don's camp when he came to me and told me that I was going to fight Larry Holmes. Don liked me, even though he had to play it like he didn't. We used to get along really well; we would sit and talk about boxing and we got on really good. It was funny because you had boxers, promoters and managers, suing each other through the court and stuff, and some of them would sit in the same bar in the evening and drink together. I remember Don coming to me and telling me about this new kid they had coming through. It was Mike Tyson, of course, and Don just said he was really strong and that he was going to trouble a lot of people. I wasn't focusing on that, though. When I knew I had the fight with Larry, I was naturally doubting myself but, when Slim told me I could do it, my confidence just grew. I had won 14 fights with him so I had no reason to believe I couldn't do it; Slim told me all I had to do was listen to what he said and I could win.

When I first went to Don's camp, nobody knew me except Slim, and I trusted him. At that camp, they had boxers who had pretty girls and nice cars, and they all had money in their pockets. I had no money in my pockets but, when I got in the ring, I was able to show what I really had. I backed everything up with my actions. They had the Muhammad Ali boxing team there; there were guys like Tony Tubbs, Tony Tucker, Percell Davis, and they all had money. Everybody else was sponsored by somebody. There was another guy called Harold Smith from Reno. He was supposed to have embezzled at least 20 million bucks, and he was backing the Muhammad Ali team that came up to Deer Lake. These boxers were riding around in big cars with 30 or 40 grand in their pockets and I had nothing but I was holding my own in the camp. There was a guy there called Gene Kilroy, and he called me "cock-strong" because there weren't any girls coming near me, even though I could fight

As we got closer to the fight, Larry stepped up his torrent of abuse. It was part of the game. He was saying he was going to take my girlfriend from me; he was saying he was going to put me on welfare; he was going to kill me.

It gave me a lot of energy as I got ready for the fight. I was just a guy struggling and coming up the hard way but, by showing I could fight, I was earning people's respect. There is a classic picture of me holding a plate and laughing with Muhammad Ali, which was taken around this time in training. The joke was Ali saying "Yo Tim, you ain't gonna get all your money from Don" and he was right. It really didn't sink into my head at the time because I was just focusing. Larry was trying to reach Rocky Marciano's record of 49 fights undefeated but, after the fight with me, he said he wasn't fighting any more young guys, and I think Greg Page was lined up for him next. This is how the IBF was created – Larry went to Bob Lee and they set it up. He thought Don King was trying to get him bumped off at one point by putting him in the ring with all these younger guys. This is why they did it. It gave Larry the chance to choose who his opponents were, but it was in his 49th fight that he lost for the very first time and Marciano's record has stayed safe to this day. It was against Michael Spinks in Vegas; they fought again six months later, and Spinks came out on top again. After that, Larry was beaten by Tyson in 1988, and that was the end of the road for him as the champ. He fought Evander Holyfield in 1992, in a bout to unify the WBC, WBA, and IBF titles, but he was 42 years old at that time and Holyfield won it.

When we got to Vegas for the fight, in May 1983, my daughter Linette, her mother Linda, and her grandmother also flew in. Somebody put them in a room of our hotel, where Larry Holmes had the whole floor. I was in the lobby with my brother Bernard, checking in, when I heard someone saying there was fight happening on the 14th floor, which is where my daughter was. We ran right up there and all of this commotion was happening, and we saw my other brother Anthony up there fighting with Larry Holmes's brother. We went up and it all got broke up. Then we went into the room where my daughter was, and, all of a sudden, I heard somebody really banging on the door. I opened it and there was Larry Holmes and his bodyguard, and Larry was shouting "Get them the hell off this floor", so I tried to go at him. My daughter's grandmother – her name was Cecilia – was pushing them both back and shouting "Get back" so I stopped and I said: "Larry – me and you; right now; downstairs." After all of the bullshit I had endured from him, I just lost my cool. It was then that I noticed him put his head down – it was only for a second – and he said "Just get them off this floor" and that was it.

This did my confidence a world of good because that's when I knew that he was scared of me a little bit. Then I got pushed back into the room and I said "Where's Linette?" and I found her underneath the bed, trembling; she was really nervous for about a week after that and we had to break her out of it. In the end, we got them into another room. I think the fight was about a week away, maybe a week-and-a-half. A couple of days later, the news show 60 Minutes had their cameras out as Larry was coming down the hall, and we were all standing there. Larry walked right up close to me and he's shouting: "I'm gonna knock him out, I have no respect for him." So I shouted: "We can do it here, right now!" The cameras were rolling and I was serious. Mitch Green and David Bay (who are Raiders of Boxing) were standing there with me, and we were ready to go, but Larry just kept on running his mouth as he walked on by

There was another incident where Larry had someone

in the back of the room, looking at me whilst I was working out. So I said "Where's Larry?" and the guy said he didn't know what I was talking about. Somebody told me he was outside, looking in and checking out how I was. I told the guy to tell him he could sit in the front row and watch me train if he wanted to because I was ready for him and I was going to knock him out. A day before this, I'm going for a work-out and I saw Larry, who took a towel and it hit me in my face. I reacted to Larry and I said "I'm gonna knock you out" but my younger brother Bernard said "No you're not; fuck that; save it for the ring" and he threw the towel back and it hit Larry in the face. Then he started fighting with Larry's younger brother and, in the end, everybody was brawling in front of the cameras and they broke that up.

I was the underdog for the fight and everybody was expecting me to get knocked out. Then Slim pulled a trick to get Larry mad and lose his focus; this is why you have got to have a good trainer. We were in the dressing-room and Slim had got to go over and watch Larry get his hands taped, and their guy had to watch me. Slim went over there first. He liked to play mind games; he was very intelligent. He told them they had too much tape on Larry's hands and made them do it again. This made Larry really mad and took him out of his mind-set a little bit. The official made Larry take the tape off and they re-wrapped the glove. Larry turned to Slim and he said: "We'll take the tape off but don't you ever say another word to me for as long as you're black."

So I'm walking out to the arena; I've got my hands up and I'm ready for him. Oh yes – I was ready to take on the great Larry Holmes. If you watch the fight, you will see that I was mentally and physically primed. Just look at my eyes. When the bell rung, the first round was very significant because that's when you can really tell who's who and what's what. I went straight to him and I was right on him because there was no respect. Right after the end of the round, I threw my hands down and I was saying "Is that all that he's got?" I kept saying "I got you, I got you" just like Ali did and I wasn't intimidated by Larry at all. The commentators say the same thing.

I kept on my front foot during those opening exchanges; I kept slipping the jab and really going at him for all as was worth. Most of what he threw at me early on was against my gloves. At one point, I remember putting my arms up beside me and taunting him. He kept coming in quick and fast but, from early on, I was protecting my head and frustrating him. The way I blocked punches was pretty unique –I used to keep my right hand planted on the left side of my face just like Slim had showed me, and it worked really well. Sugar Ray Robinson used to do that and he would intimidate people. It kind of became one of my trademarks. I just remember smiling the biggest smile when that bell ended and I couldn't wait for the next round. Every round after that, I think I won, but there was that amazing ninth round which everybody talks about; it was voted the round of the year, and I think it was also voted the best ninth round ever.

During that round, I heard all the screaming and I was thinking: "Wow, I've got Larry Holmes hurt!" I was hearing the crowd and, for a second, I couldn't believe where I was and what I was doing – I was on my way to being the Heavyweight Champion of the World. In the opening stages, I hit him three or four times in the face and I hurt him on the side of his head with my right hand. Then I hit him again, three of four times, and I had him against the ropes and he was struggling. When you look at the footage, Larry looks totally out of it, and I was going in for the kill when the referee came in and broke us apart. With one minute thirty of the round left, I opened up on Larry again with the last of my strength and the crowd went absolutely crazy. He looked like he was going down but he just held on for all he was worth and survived until the end, even getting a few bruising shots at me, most of which I took on the gloves. My punches were the kind of power-shots that will put any man on their ass, but Larry stood tall, and I could have done with that extra five per cent that people like Tyson and Holyfield had because of their supreme conditioning and obsession with training. Nevertheless, I knew Larry was hanging on by his finger nails.

I went back to the corner and everyone was pumping me saying "Come on Tim, you got to do what you got to do" and the crowd were on my side. Every round, I was in his chest because of all the stuff he had put me through. There were a couple of rounds in there when I danced like Ali, especially towards the end, and the crowd loved it as I threw out jabs like a crazy guy. I felt good because I knew I had the fight. Then we get to the last round, I danced again, and outpunched him and made him look bad. Then the bell rang and – boom! – I threw my hands up into the air and stood directly in front of his corner. I was thinking, before the fight, if I win, they weren't going to give it to me unless I knocked him out because of who I was. Larry Holmes put in so much that they weren't about to let him slip, plus the fact that Don was the promoter and they were after Marciano's record. I was really mad when they awarded it to him and you can see that in my interview at the end. When he heard the verdict,

Larry changed his tune, but he knew he had taken a beating. I wasn't totally unsurprised at the result but it's just a shame that the paying public were, I think, deceived. The actions of that contest rippled outwards and affected us all. In the end, I was forced to throw a fight to get away from it all, but all I ever wanted to do was box and take my chances. The best thing to come from the fight against Larry Holmes was the fact that I put a whooping on him, and now, of course, people knew who I was.

Chapter Nine

The King and the Champion

AFTER the Larry Holmes fight, I told the media that he was just holding that belt for me because I was going to take it from him and I don't think there were a lot of people then who didn't agree. I had proved myself and I was one of the top contenders, but I had to put the defeat to the back of my mind and not let it beat me up, because I believed I knew the truth about the fight. The more I thought about it, and went around the world listening to people, the more I knew I had won it. I had to move on, though. I had a real belief that I could be the champion of the world but I knew Don wasn't going to give me a rematch with Larry, and I don't think Larry wanted it either. When I left the arena, everybody was disappointed and they were shouting: "Bullshit! Bullshit! Bullshit!" Back at the hotel, people were giving me so much respect; they couldn't believe the way the decision went. But I was happy. I did a good job. I was pleased with myself, but I got robbed.

That's the way boxing is, I suppose, and, later on, I became friends with Larry. Even after the fight, there was still a lot of tension and animosity. Lightning Bob Smith lived in South Philly and I was like an older, bigger, brother to him. I used to teach him how to do stuff in the ring and that's how my jaw got broken. I was showing him how to pull a left hook whilst we were sparring and he hit me and it broke. He bet Larry's brother, Mark Holmes, a big amount of money that I would win the fight so they had that going on. After the fight, we were at the party and Lightning Bob walked over to Mark and said: "You know that we won, why don't you pay up?" Larry's brother hit him with an overhand right but Bob took it well, even though his blood was trickling down the walls. I had my back to them, pushing and shoving with Larry's bodyguard, Big Bobby D, and when I turned around, I saw Bob and I said to him: "What did you do?" He said "I just went over there and asked him for the money", and we were all set to go over there and fight but then I thought about it and I knew Don would never give me another shot if we did. So I said "No", and I made everybody leave, and we went and had our own party.

We flew back to Philly and everybody in the neighbourhood was waiting to greet me when the limo pulled up and we got out. People were standing in their doors and I was a proud man. I put all the luggage in my mom's house, and I was really touched by it all. Then we got into the car and left. I was my neighbourhood hero and that meant a lot to me. This is all a long time ago now so I don't want to dwell too much about what could have been – I know there are thousands of boxers and sportsmen out there who feel like they have been robbed, but what can you do? All I would say to people is: watch that fight against

Larry and score it yourself. Larry was a great fighter; even when it looked like he was about to fall, somehow he just kept on going. I know in my heart of hearts what really happened that day.

There was another fighter in our camp called Mitch Green; he was from Queens in New York and he'd been with Don King longer than anyone. Everybody loves Mitch; he is a cool dude, and he's a Raider; he's one of us. Everybody was getting title shots before him – me, Greg Page, Tony Tubbs, and David Bey – and in my opinion that's what caused him to start going crazy. Mitch was my friend. We talked every day and trained and sparred together. He was such a tough man and he had so much heart; he went ten rounds with Mike Tyson. Things were pretty bad for us heavyweights then, and that's why I spent some time in the UK, away from things. I also spent some time in the US with Mitch and we were okay; I have nothing bad to say about his game. I even tried to tell him about Don, and that I didn't think we should fight each other because we were in the same boat. There was also talk about me getting in the ring with Tyson for $500,000, but other fighters were getting a couple of million and I wasn't going to do it for a quarter of that. We used to sit there in camp and it would be good natured most of the time; Mitch would be telling me jokes, and that's why I started to like him.

It wasn't just what other people were doing that stopped the development of my family and my kids – it was me as well. Before I got into the kind of life I was leading, I was a clean-living guy. Then I started drinking and partying and smoking dope, and doing a little bit of cocaine, so I'm not going to blame it all on others. I should have managed my money properly and I should have been more aware of what I had. You could have given me $50m and it would have probably been the same, but then I have too many friends and family around me that wouldn't have let me lose that amount of cash. Look at Tyson – he told me he had $319m when he got out of jail, and he ended up broke. I should have been a man and took care of my own affairs. I guess I learned the hard way. I would say my biggest purse was about a million bucks. I know, if I had been marketed properly, I could have made a lot more, but Don King Productions didn't promote individual boxers.

When I was growing up, the Philly Muslims were around us. They were good guys although you wouldn't want to cross them because they looked after their own just like everybody else did – the Italians and the Irish did, and we did, too. They encouraged a lot of blacks not to eat pork and to live a clean life; if you did something wrong, they would discipline you for it. They had a lot to do with boxing in the city, and they had a lot to do with the growth of the young blacks. They did a lot for us when we were little. They helped some of the boxers later on because they weren't afraid of Don and they would stand against him. There was one time when they went to his office and they demanded $10,000 they claimed he owed, and they got it out of him and divided it up. There was another time when they went to Don's house and his wife was at home alone; if she had opened the door, there could have been big trouble.

There was another guy, a legendary guy, called Jeremiah Shabazz, who was a powerful man in the city and he helped us. It was Jeremiah who convinced Muhammad Ali to change his name from Cassius Clay and became his confidant.

Jeremiah was also involved with Malcolm X when he was younger and he and Malcolm worked closely together for several years. Malcolm was a minister in Philadelphia and Jeremiah was East Coast Captain, both in the Nation of Islam. All we had to do was go and ask him for some advice when we felt threatened, or when bad things were going on. We called him "The Old Man"; we would have a meeting with him and then we would know exactly what to do. He became Ali's top aide in the early 1970s. He was officially Ali's administrative assistant and most people who came to Ali about business had to go through Jeremiah. In fact, that's how Don met Ali. He came up to the camp one day, wanting to speak to the champ. Ali's security quickly surrounded him before Jeremiah came out to speak to Don. I have heard stories about Don trying to get really close to Ali, but he had to deal with Jeremiah instead. Although Jabir Herbert Muhammad – son of the leader of the Nation of Islam, the Honorable Elijah Muhammad – was Ali's boxing manager, Jeremiah was very important in the everyday decisions Ali made regarding other business. When Tom Hauser wrote The Life and Times of Muhammad Ali, Jeremiah acted as consultant.

Later, Jeremiah provided information for HBO Movies when they produced Only in America, which was the movie about Don's rise to fame. Some of that information was controversial; about Don paying Ali $50,000 to abandon a lawsuit against him for fraud, for example. I think the Thrilla in Manila was the championship fight in question. Ali said that Don had deliberately failed to pay him the million dollars which was a part of their total contractual agreement. Shabazz said he acted in good faith when he was given $50,000 by Don to pay Ali. Don claimed that he instructed Jeremiah to only give Ali the money if he signed a waiver saying he was dropping all legal proceedings. After receiving the money, Ali said he thought it was a down payment on the million Don owed him. Don said he gave Ali the cash to drop the lawsuit. This became a bone of contention and Jeremiah was in the middle and seen by some to have sold Ali out for $25,000 which Don allegedly gave him for services rendered. This caused a split between Don and Jeremiah but those who knew Jeremiah understood it to be another of Don's tricks. This time he went too far, and Don received a visit from the FBI telling him they had intercepted messages from unknown sources, threatening his life. Don had two choices: to go into FBI protection or try to find out who was trying to kill him. For this task, he needed someone who knew the streets and all of the players. There was only one man he knew that could put this whole dirty business behind him – he called Jeremiah Shabazz. Having no knowledge of the situation, Jeremiah recommended that Don hire Yusef Shah, who was formally the East Coast Captain of the Nation of Islam and was known by many as the Shah of New York. All of Don's worries seemed to gradually disappear and he retained Captain Yusef as his permanent advisor.

Don King entered the boxing world by storm and his history is already in the public domain. He was an ex-convict and numbers banker, and he went to prison for second degree murder after he kicked a man's head in for not paying a debt. He is what we call connected and, for this reason, he was able to keep fighters in line and use money to buy people's loyalty. Having said this, you can see how easy it was for him to buy me from Mark Stewart for peanuts because he was new to the game and was on his way to jail, so he was trying to liquidate his assets. Don bought a contract for five fights and he told me to sign it; the contract was blank, so he was able to do whatever he wanted. When I look back at it, although Slim was good to me, Don used the relationship I had with him because it was Slim who told me this was how business in boxing was done and that I should keep my mouth shut; but, of course, he was on pay-roll. Also, Don owned the Monarch Boxing management company and he made his stepson Carl the president. You could not fight for Don King Promotions unless you signed with Monarch Boxing, who received 50 per cent of my earnings, and I had to pay Don for promoting my fight, which was a clear conflict of interests. My cousin, Murad Ziyad, saw Don put the numbers $80,000 on to my signed contract just for the use of his training camp, and that is just the tip of the iceberg.

Well, things soon went crazy because, when you go from being broke to what we call "nigger rich", you have absolutely no idea how to handle your money. Every heavyweight champ, from Jack Dempsey to Jack Johnson, was extravagant. Like I said, Larry Holmes rented a whole floor at the Riviera Hotel just to fight a kid by the name of Tim Witherspoon. In fact, this kind of exhibitionism has been in the sport since the very beginning. Heavyweight champions are looked at as immortals, so money is no object to the fighter. Although the promoter makes it available, he's going to get every dime back off the top, and this is where the problem was with me and Don. Looking back, I wasn't fully understanding of the situation that all the expenses were coming out of the purse. Most promoters make it separate when they are dealing with a champion and, if you look at the fight, I had with Pinklon Thomas, I was only getting around $400,000, and that was down to about $80,000 by the time the bell rang. I had paid for about 30 people to fly into Vegas for that fight, including some ladies who had their own private suites, and all those 30 people were doubled up in rooms. Pinklon was doing the same as me, and his logo "Think Pink" seemed to be everywhere. There was a little bit of friction and my brother Anthony had run-ins with Pinklon and his crew almost on a daily basis. It was Angelo Dundee who kept me and Pink from going for it before the fight at the casino and this made Don as mad as hell because it made him look like he didn't have any control over us. There had already been a small riot at his training camp and I think his strategy was to control me through Aaron Snowell and Slim, and it wasn't working. That's when it really started to get crazy and I called Jeremiah Shabazz and Yusef Shah for some advice, and I was told to be cool and save my energy for the ring. In spite of everything, Don had made a good point – he told the Press that he took a bunch of guys who were hardly paid anything and gave them a chance to become millionaires.

The next man I fought after Larry was Floyd Cummings, from Mississippi. He had been doing really well until he came up against Renaldo Snipes two years before we go it on in the summer of 1983; he'd had 14 wins, and 12 of them were by KO. After that, it all went to hell for him. He won one more, then he drew against Joe Frazier in his last ever fight which was a comeback fight six years after a grilling from George Foreman that ended with him being TKO'd in the fifth round. Before our fight, Floyd he had been defeated three times in a row, but we had a good hard fight which all three referees had me down as a win, and I got a unanimous decision. Floyd was well built, and he was a strong fighter.

After I beat him, he took on Frank Bruno and he nearly knocked him out in the first round but Frank was saved by the bell. In the end, Bruno came back and he won by TKO in the seventh, and that was the last fight Floyd ever had. After I beat him, I knew I had worked hard. I also knew I had to work even harder if I was going to win that championship, but I was still convinced I could do it, and everyone else in the camp was telling me I could do it.

I was over the Larry Holmes fight, and now they were lining me up against James "Quick" Tillis, which was a re-arrangement. The fight had originally been called off because I had an ear infection and, on that occasion, Don got me to come down to Cleveland to explain it all to the Media. I had a letter from my doctor saying that the infection was serious and that it could affect my balance but, when I got there, they had another doctor and he was telling me I was clear to fight, and they tried to make me. In the end I said "No", but this is the way they would operate, and then, of course, you would get your punishment for fucking up the plan. Of course, I knew there was an agenda with him and, as I was stepping further away from the inner circle, the screws got tighter. Those early fights, when I was with Mark Stewart, is where he saw my potential as a fighter who would take it up the ass. But he was wrong.

I was raring to go for the Quick Tillis fight and I went to town on him and knocked him out in the first round; it took me just over two minutes. The fight was for the vacant North American Boxing Federation title, and I remember it took place in Richfield, Ohio. Things had turned sour with me and Don by now but you have to remember there were other boxers who were having problems with him. One of those was Greg Page, who was arguing and fighting with him, so I kind of laid back and I said to myself: "Wait a minute." I decided I was going to be cool and not start anything with him about the money. As I said earlier, Larry Holmes didn't want to fight any more young guys so they went away and set up the IBF, which left the WBC belt vacant, and myself and Greg were the top contenders at the time. Because Greg had been arguing and fighting with Don, I knew that he would have to do extra work to beat me, so I got in good shape. I knew the judges and everybody would be on my side for this one because Greg was running his mouth to the Press, which gave me the advantage

Before the fight, they tried to play tricks. They told me Greg had been talking to my girlfriend, so I ran downstairs and confronted him. He told me he wasn't trying to talk to her and he got scared of me. He was a great guy and I liked him a lot. He died a couple of years back. He collapsed after his last fight and was hospitalized with a massive bleed on his brain. He suffered a stroke and was in a coma for a week or so, and he had complications for the rest of his life. He filed a lawsuit because the fight referee wasn't licensed and there wasn't an ambulance, paramedics, or even any oxygen at the venue, which is against the law. They've now got a set of boxing initiatives that have been operation for almost a decade, and they called those laws the Greg Page Safety Initiative in memory of him. Greg held the WBA Championship for a couple months in the mid-1980s and his death was really terrible.

Our fight took place in the Convention Centre in Vegas in March 1984. It was a close fight and Greg had the advantage of being bigger and faster than me, and he came at me from the very first second. He was dancing and moving around the ring, but I picked my shots and defended myself well. I got a couple of good combinations in, and I hit him with a right which snapped his head back in that opening round and I knew I could take him. I kept my nerve and tried to stick to everything my trainers had taught me, even though I was mad with everything going on around me. I had that in common with Greg. I did well at pinning him to the ropes but, in the eighth round, he started to come at me and I took the heat out of it by hitting him in the head as much as I could during the last two or three rounds. In the 11th, I hit him with a left, and then a right, and I thought he was going to fall. Then, in the last round, I must have hit him with six or seven head shots and I think he was glad when the bell went, but I also think he knew I had won it. In the end, they gave me the decision and that is how I won the WBC Heavyweight Championship of the World.

Chapter Ten

Think Pink

AFTER I became the WBC Heavyweight Champion of the World, I didn't really feel like a champ. I went home with about $40,000, which left a sour taste in my mouth. I would never know what I was going to pick up after a fight, and that was a problem. We were never allowed to ask Don how much we were going to get; if we did, we would be accused of starting trouble, and we'd feel frozen out of things. His son Carl did try to help us boxers. He would come in and drink with us after training and he would say "I wish my father would do the right thing sometimes" and he would have tried to change the way we were treated if he could. Yes, in some respects, he was like a puppet, but he did try to make things better. He said to a lot of us boxers that he was going to try to get his father to give us more money. Then, when he was with his father, he had to act like he was 100 per cent behind him. It didn't work out, but he did try to help us out.

There were a lot of people who loved me when I was coming up, and I had some of them tell me I reminded them of Ali because of the way I helped out so many strangers and didn't take care of myself. I am older and wiser now, but if you saw the way I was robbed when I was younger, it would make you cry. Most boxers have been hit in the head so much they can't recall the bullshit from the harsh reality. A lot of them are broke or they live in homeless shelters; they have no pensions, no insurance or union. Some have mental problems, and some are in prison. Boxing has not changed much since 1920, when Jack Johnson took a dive against Jess Willard to have charges of white slavery dismissed. They broke me because Tyson was the next big ticket. There really is no difference between pit-bull fighting and pro boxing; to the promoter, we are just animals. Have you seen Tyson's one-man act on HBO? It's pathetic, a great champion reduced to nothing. He makes a fool out of himself, running around on stage with a wig on to make people laugh while Don lives off the millions he made from him. My story is every boxer's story. People like Joe Louis, Sugar Ray Robinson, Sonny Liston all had no money; there were very few who came away with what they actually earned.

Something happened between the Larry Holmes fight and the Pinklon Thomas fight. I know I was causing a stink and complaining about not getting paid but my relationship with Don was soured because of the way he was treating me. My cousin Murad always had my back, even before I got into boxing and, if I had any trouble, then he would sort it out for me. I do not know if there was a direct threat to me when the court case started, but there were wolves out there. It was the fight against Larry that created the hostility in me, but I felt other fighters were being ripped off by Don, too, and I just didn't want to fight for him any more; it was as simple as that. There was so much anger because I thought Don had pulled a number on everybody. Okay, so I was naïve; I had a lot of people telling me I would get the money I was entitled to. Even Ali had said it to me but I think we both knew I wasn't going to get my full money. I just didn't think it would be as bad as it was.

The fight against Larry was my first real big-money fight and, if I had been paid what I thought was right, it would have got me out of the hole I was in and put me on solid ground. I think I was supposed to get around $125,000, and I went home with only $65,000, which made things difficult for me. Most of the boxers got a wage and Carl King would come over on a Friday and pay everybody. Most of the time, people in the camp were broke after living the lavish lifestyle and burning up their money. I was like a loan shark; I was giving guys money until payday. So I was like the leader, in a way. I was the good guy, and a lot of them gave me respect and looked up to me and we were all cool. Michael Dokes was the only one who was a separatist. He was on his own and Don treated him different to everybody else and gave him what he wanted. He had his own little cabin, but he was still cool with us all. So, Carl had the wages and was supposed to pay the boxers, but, one time, they couldn't find him; a bunch of the guys went down to his house to get paid but he wouldn't answer the door. Don has a huge estate and Carl's house is in there. We had gone down to Carl's house to collect the money that they get every Friday – I went with them even though I had money – but no-one answered the door. They kept on knocking, but there was no answer, so we left and came back to the camp without any money. When the other boxers heard about this, about 20 of us got in our cars and drove back up there. Bernard Hopkins' uncle Arty McCloud was there, too. No-one answered, but we knew someone was in the house. So we came back from Carl's house for the second time and we were really mad. When we got back to the camp, I took a trash can and threw it through the window. I don't know why I did it. Then everybody got guns and they started shooting at electrical boxes and making holes in the ceilings of the brand new dormitories; they even started shooting at animals. The Sheriff was called to rectify the situation and he pulled his gun on my brother Stevie.

When it was all over, Don flew in from Vegas and he was as mad as hell. He had everybody come before him one at a time. The verdict was you either stayed with no money, or you got kicked out. He told my brother Stevie that he had to go, and he told Arty and a lot of people that they were leaving. A real wall of hatred was building up, with a lot of people against Don, but there was nobody of any real power who would stand up against him then. He had the Sheriff going up there, checking on his property, and he was able to call on him when all hell broke out with us. I remember Stevie pulling a knife and the Sheriff said he would shoot him if he came at him. It was a really scary moment for me because I love my brother, and he was only doing what he thought was right to get money he felt was his.

Even though things died down for a time, it was all going to go crazy when I got the lawsuit against Don underway, and my cousin Murad eventually found out there was a threat against me. People were apparently going to hurt me if I didn't co-operate; they wanted me to stop complaining about what I was getting paid; and they wanted me to drop the lawsuit. Watch the HBO movie on Don – it shows you some of the stuff I was dealing with. I was living it every day and I had to keep looking over my shoulder. With the drugs and all the other things I was doing, I was really scared; I didn't know who was lurking in the shadows ready to pull a knife or a gun out on me. I was living with the idea that I could be murdered, but I also knew I had to stick up for what I believed, what was right, and I had bills to pay. I just wanted my money but, before that, I would have to get down on my hands and knees and say I was sorry and tell the Press I was just making trouble, and they printed my stories even though they knew deep down I was telling the truth.

Before the fight against Pinklon, I felt like I was being interrogated by the officials from the WBC. Jose Sulaiman was one of them. They took me into a room and I felt they treated me like they were policemen trying to put pressure on their prisoner. Of course, they were friends of Don. As I said, things had been building up since the Larry Holmes fight and, although I was trying to play it cool before I fought Greg Page, I could feel the pressure in my head now, and I was starting to get depressed. I began to drink beer, smoke marijuana and use cocaine, although I would leave it out when I was training for the fights. I was not some kind of hoodlum when I was a youngster, as everyone will tell you; I was an athlete, pretty much a clean-living guy. Tommy Wade eventually found out exactly what I was doing and I can remember hearing the disappointment in his voice. Apart from trying coke one time, I did not do drugs when I was growing up; it's only when I started moving in those circles where such things were readily available that I got more involved.

I fought Pinklon Thomas on August 31, 1984, just after the Olympics had finished in LA, and Tyrell Biggs had won the gold in the super-heavyweight division. I was getting ready to fight, but I felt Don and his people were pulling against me. My head felt like it was going sideways; I was not in a good place, and people were starting to notice. I had bought the shop, which my father and sister were running while I was upstairs in the apartment, taking cocaine. I was still keeping it together at that point because I was still fighting, but that was all going to change. It wasn't long until we would be starting to hear the name Mike Tyson. Don was consumed by promoting him when he signed him in 1988, but I didn't meet him when he first started out. He was just some kid who was up and coming and I don't think anybody could have predicted what he was going to do in the boxing world. He was a great fighter, but there was an agenda for him to become the youngest Heavyweight Champion of the World. His first professional fight took place in March 1985 against Hector Mercedes; a year and a half later, he beat Trevor Berbick to become the WBC heavyweight champ when he was 20 years old.

Murad was approached by some people and he was told he could make some money by doing a job for them. All he had to do was go up to the camp and shake the boxers up so they would stay quiet. But these people didn't know that he was my cousin. He also saw the contract Don had given me after all of the trouble; Don had totalled up massive expenses, and charged me through the roof for training and everything else I had used. He would order the fighters to be at camp, and then he would charge them for their trouble; you were paying for everything, all of the time. I overheard a guy speaking one time. He was saying: "Yeah, that Tim

Witherspoon – he was always borrowing money off of Don, so there's two sides to every story" I felt like punching him on the nose. Sure, you could go to Don or Carl and maybe get a few grand if you were down on your luck and Don was in a good mood, but there is no way that any boxing promoter in the world will lend a fighter hundreds of thousands, or millions, of dollars, against his next fight. It just doesn't happen.

    In the beginning, Don came into boxing through Muhammad Ali and Jeremiah Shabazz, really good guys who so many people looked up to. Murad worked for Jeremiah. None of them were thugs – they were respected and they had respect – but, like I say, they were like a force of nature and would band together if they ever came under attack. I never got involved with the wrong sort of people. I knew them, but I was never in their pockets because I knew myself and my family could get hurt. I started to wise up to it all and Jeremiah taught me a lot about the ways of the world, and gave me advice on how I could deal with situations, especially with Don because he knew how he worked. The people I had against me knew I was a nice guy and they wanted to intimidate me; I felt I couldn't even make a complaint to the officials because everybody was with Don. You could always tell when a fighter was going to win a fight because Don would go and stand by him.

    Don wanted Pinklon to beat me and he hired Angelo Dundee to work with him and give him the best training he could get. It was strange that Slim mysteriously disappeared when I was getting ready for the fight, which meant I was at a big disadvantage straight away. A boxer fights by ear, more than by hand, and Slim had always been there throughout my fights, constantly telling me what to do. Without that voice in the ring, I couldn't really see the way forward. I couldn't see how I was going to beat Pinklon because Slim was withdrawn at the last minute. After every round, I was coming back to the corner and my team were saying: "Tim, you're not doing enough; you've got to up your game if you're going to win." Slim said he disappeared because Don wasn't paying me, but I believe it was done on purpose because they wanted to put me at a disadvantage, and they certainly did that. I ended up with Aaron Snowell as my trainer for that fight and, to be honest, I knew more about training than him because, like I said earlier, he wasn't in the game and he never boxed himself.

The fight itself was at the Rivera Hotel in Vegas; and my cousin Murad came up with the lawyer Nate Carabello, Lee Beloff, and other well-respected Philly guys. There were also two lawyers from Washington DC who wanted to start a sports management firm. One of them told me that the corruption in boxing was so bad that they wanted to protect it from unscrupulous promoters and that investing any money into it was going to make you a loss. I was starting to figure that out for myself. Nate was also from south Philly, and he took an interest in boxing because he and Lee grew up together and they were friends. Lee was also an attorney and a Philadelphian City councilman, and they had some good ideas. Murad had already signed a contract with them to help promote a fighter and to keep all the taxes right, but I was paranoid and I didn't trust them at first.

These guys were top-of-the-line lawyers from DC and they had connections, too, and Murad convinced me that they were okay. I already had a lawyer, but I did begin to trust them, although an interview with one of their associates for a Vegas newspaper annoyed me. He made it sound like boxers were incompetent and threw their money around like confetti. I was angry because I had taken them out to lunch and they had watched me blow a lot of money on tips and on my entourage. None of these guys were small-time operators and I know Murad hired Nate to get a fighter out of a gun charge in Philly. He was clean, but he knew all the players. Lee Beloff's father was a judge; my uncle, Gally Witherspoon, drove for him for years until he retired. I stayed friends with Nate and the others, and Lee was like family. I listened to him and he came to my room and we talked, but I had already hired Marc Risman to represent me.

Murad was managing a junior-middleweight and I said it would be okay for them to come up and get some publicity for him from my fight. He brought the lawyers up with him to let Don know that, if he pulled anything, then they would take care of it. If he tried anything outside of the law, maybe after the fight, or outside, then Murad and his people would take care of that, too. I was protected and I knew Don would not fuck with these guys. They were giving him the message that they were there for me and, if he set his dogs on me, they were going to come at him.

Throughout the fight, all Pink did was throw his jab, but it wasn't as good as Larry Holmes'. If I knew beforehand that he was left-handed, it would have been a different fight. I handled Larry pretty well, as I said earlier, but you're only as good as your team working together. Pinklon had Angelo Dundee in his corner and I had Aaron. Aaron had an idea of what to do because he was in my corner since my first fight, but I was depending on my skills and what Slim had showed me. If Aaron had seen something I needed to know, he would tell me, but it wasn't the same as having Slim there with me. I also had Sugar Ray Leonard's cuts man Eddie Aliano, who was the best he business; he was from south Philly, too. He took care of me when I got back to the corner, but I knew I had to knock Pinklon out because the cards were stacked against me. I fought the fight a champion would fight; I kept the jab moving and I kept going for his body. I hurt his ribs whilst he was busy throwing his jab as hard as he could. To my recollection, he also threw some body shots; he wasn't running from me and we were trying to get him to exchange punches, which he would not do. I knew his ribs were hurt, and we basically stood in the middle of the ring at times and tried to out jab one another. There was no dancing around or avoiding punches; we just hit each other hard. If you are the contender and you are trying to take the belt off the champ, you have got to do more than just throw jabs. Despite the disadvantage of not having Slim there, I still didn't think I was at risk of being stopped or knocked out by Pinklon, and I hit him so hard in the first round that I made his face swell up.

When Slim finally appeared weeks after the fight, he claimed he had no money. In spite of everything, I looked out for him. Like I say, I loved him even though I knew he was a player. You have to remember that he made me into the boxer I am, even if he did play me and Don in the end.

I can also remember seeing Slim and Mark Stewart talking before Mark went to jail, and I think they were trying to get something on Don, but Don didn't trust Slim because of the way he was. He was sneaky and Don cut his money from something like $2,000 dollars to about $500. He came to

Still "Terrible"

My brothers Bernard and Steve, and me

With my crew, waiting for Tommy Wade

Playing baseball for South Philly High

Playing football for South Philly High - number 84

How did Larry Holmes stay on his feet?

Lay your hand on my shoulder, Larry

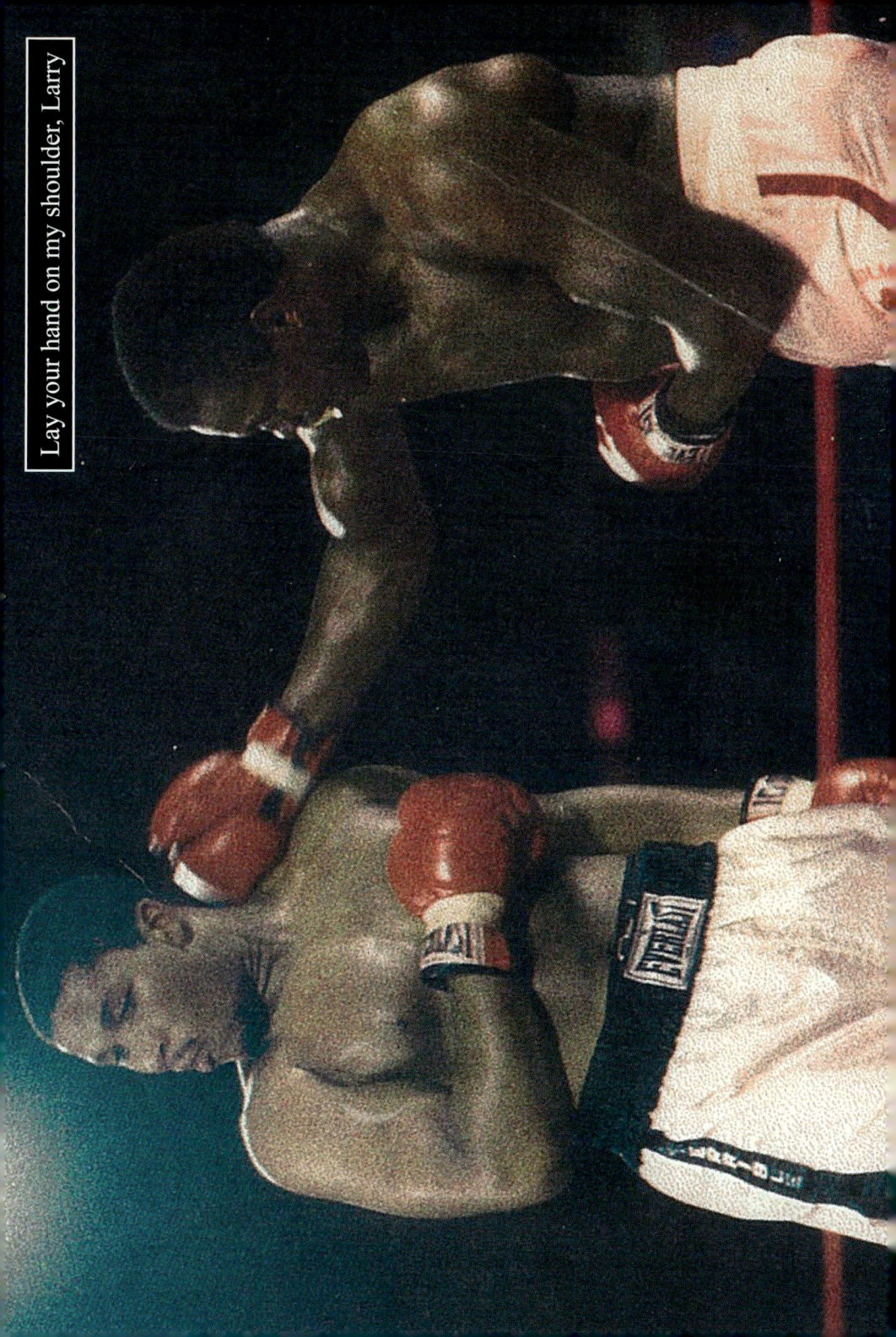

WBC Champion in 1984 after beating Greg Page

Winning the WBA title against Tony Tubbs in 1986

On the way to beating Frank Bruno

Getting ready to throw the heavyweight Championship of the World against James "Bonecrusher" Smith

On the "Rocky" steps

Those famous steps in Philadelphia, again, where Rocky Balboa did his thing - I'm in the middle, taking a group of European hopefuls to the art museum

My kids: Ayanna, Tim Junior, Indya, Mecca, and Linette

I can do smart!

True Vindication!

A proud moment - being inducted into the Pennysylvania Boxing Hall of Fame

Presented To
TIM WITHERSPOON
Congratulations Upon Your Induction
Into The
**PENNSYLVANIA
BOXING HALL OF FAME**
Presented By RING ONE V.B.A
May 18, 2008

Ringside at an amateur contest in Philly in 2008

PERSONAL TRAINING

Encouraging the next generation

Calling the shots

Pine Lake

me in the dorms, crying, and he said: "Tim, I'm gonna shoot this mutherfucker if he don't give me my money." I know he would have done it because Slim was a bounty-hunter. He had his guns on him and everything, and he told me he had to leave else he was going to shoot him. I told him not to, but he split after a couple days, right before the fight. Don cut him down because he thought he was a big snake, and he also knew I would be at a great disadvantage without him in my corner. I knew the only way I was going to retain my belt and stay as the champ was if I knocked Pinklon out, but he managed to stay on his feet and, in the end, he won the fight by the majority decision.

It is, of course, a matter of life or death in the ring, and a good trainer will help you keep your mind clear and stop you from being confused. Without Slim in there with me, I knew I had to go for it and try and find that knockout punch but, without that guidance, I might as well have gone into the ring with one arm tied behind my back. A trainer will relay certain information to the promoter; he might say to him "Yeah, I've got his mind" and whoever has the fighter's mind is who the promoter wants to deal with. Pinklon was a strong challenger but I do not think he did enough to take that belt off me. I don't think he raised his game enough to be challenging for the Heavyweight Championship of the World, but then he knew he just had to stay on his feet and the rest would be taken care of.

Chapter Eleven

Turning the Screw

BEFORE I fought Pinklon, I had been pretty vocal about what Don had been doing. I'd been talking to the newspapers and the TV stations and, in the end, a message was sent for me to stop. But I didn't stop. It was then that I was told I was only going to win if I knocked Pinklon out, and they were going to make sure of that. It started out with me getting messages; then I started getting visitors, I think the first one was José Sulaiman. He told me that if I did not start to co-operate with Don, I was going to get suspended and that I would never fight again. There were lawyers; people from the commission; even Don's right-hand man Duke Durden came in and threatened me. They all tried to tell me to stop blasting Don, but I kept on because I thought he was taking my money. I didn't know any better; everyone else kept their mouth closed and I didn't. If I had kept quiet, I still don't think it would have been any different for me because I was from Philly. Don didn't trust me, or anyone from Philly, and there was that link with Slim and

Mark Stewart (with Slim probably passing Mark messages) and I was always going to be the outsider. Don also knew the situation with the Muslims and that I was cool with all of those guys, even the ones who were in the prison who had never met me. When Don got beat up in the Bahamas and everyone was threatening him, I think I got the after-effects of that. But, even though we didn't trust one another, I couldn't help liking the guy and I was hoping he would change.

Almost every day leading up to the Pinklon fight, I was being told that, if I didn't keep quiet, there was going to be trouble. I spoke to the newspapers in Vegas and told them that Don had taken my money; I just didn't care about the consequences. I was naïve and I didn't realise you've got to keep quiet if you were going to get paid and be successful. I was replaceable, it was as simple as that – Don had about a dozen other heavyweights in his stable. If you didn't do as he said, he would make one of the others the champion. He had them all signed up so he could control them. He was kind of playing chess with us all. I call it "All the King's Men" because it felt like we were his pawns and he kept playing with all of us. A couple of people have asked me whether or not I think Don is crazy, and to talk to him, you would have to say "No." He is very intelligent, but he uses that power to help himself. I never seen him violent and go off at people around me, but maybe he did in his loan shark, or number-running days. He appeared to me like a jolly old guy who was stealing everybody's money. I came from an area where you saw guys getting mean and screaming all the time; that was normal to me. If somebody wanted to have a fight, they would do it, and even though I wasn't involved in shooting or stabbing, I did see things that went on. My cousin Murad grew up in the same environment as me and he did the exact opposite. He started going to reformatories very early on, and then to jail, where he began to educate himself. He joined the Nation of Islam. He told me he had a straight choice between joining them or the Black Panther Party. Most of the guys he ran around with were former hustlers and gangsters, but do you know what caused him to follow the Nation of Islam? One night, we were all standing on the corner of Fifth and McKean Street and a Muslim brother named Mike Ellis was on the corner trying to sell the Muhammad Speaks newspapers. There was a gang member that didn't like what he was doing and words were exchanged and a fight started. We were watching it when someone in the crowd passed a knife to the gang member and he planted it into Michael's chest. We still talk about this sometimes – how we saw him fall and tremble, and watched as his last breath left his body. Up until then, it was a clean contest; everybody from Seventh Street could fight. The cops took their time to arrive and, by that time, Michael was dead. I didn't really get involved with all of the religious stuff but I respected them. The racial tensions ran very high in our neighborhood and white police brutality was common. After that night, my brothers and I went one way, and Murad went the other. The night Michael was killed, Murad and two corner boys waited for the ambulance which also took a long time.

In his own way, I think Don liked me because he knew I wasn't the type to go around spitting and cursing at people. Like I say, he had been having a lot of trouble in Philly and that was the problem. All I did was stand up to him; I didn't do it in a violent way – I just spoke my mind, and even when people were talking about hurting him, I told them to leave him alone. I just didn't want to deal with violence. There are so many stories from the past about boxers tangled up with promoters and they end up with no money, or they end up getting hurt, and I just didn't want it to be that way. I suffered; a lot of the boxers from my generation suffered, but we did help to make it a better world for the boxers around today. I'm not saying there isn't anybody out there not getting ripped off, but it is definitely harder for the unscrupulous to get in on it now.

I don't know if people got tired of all the stories and accusations going around, but many of them knew what I was saying was true, and I think it did work in my favour in the end; it just took a long time. All people wanted was to see a good fight for the Heavyweight Championship of the World, and I remember, when I fought Pinklon, all the other big heavyweights were fighting on the card. I had a run-in with Pink a couple of days before the fight and Angelo Dundee ended up breaking it up. We were running (I had about 20 people with me) and all of a sudden somebody said "There goes Pinklon Thomas" and he was running in the other direction, coming towards us. So, I ran up to him and I told him I was going to knock him out, and that's when I realized the guy had just as much heart as me. He didn't back down at all. He came towards me like he was ready to fight me and I knew I was in a fight. We were getting ready to push one another and throw punches and then Angelo got in the middle and told us to save it for the fight, so we did. I knew Angelo –he was born only two or three blocks away from where I was born – and I respected him.

Another thing I wasn't told was Pinklon was a southpaw. He threw a lot of jabs at me during the fight that I didn't see and they scored him points. Slim would have told me that if he had been with me and we would have practiced a lot of things just so I could have been ready for it, but I was totally unprepared for it. My head just wasn't in the game for that fight – I'd just won the title and then I lost my trainer – and I guess somebody somewhere was reporting into Don that my head wasn't in it. I had all the pressure of getting suspended and, of course, I knew I was going to lose if I did not get the KO. I felt like the world was falling in on me a little bit and it was not the greatest state of mind to be in, and I was living with these pressures every single minute. Every single day, when I had finished at the gym, I would come home and dive in the pool and swim until they said to me: "What are you doing in the water? You're fighting in a few days? Don't you know swimming takes off your strength?" I got out of that pool and I said to myself: "What am I doing?" I was swimming every day after my work-out and I wasn't supposed to be; I was supposed to be resting.

I really didn't know what I was supposed to be doing. Without guidance, I went ahead and I bought vitamin supplements to help improve my strength and give me energy, but you're not supposed to overdo it and I drunk more of it before the fight than I should have done. I tried to rest, but I noticed I was kind of fatigued as the fight got closer and I felt sluggish getting into the ring. We were in the dressing-room and I knew I had a big task in front of me, but the first couple of rounds went really well. There was a little bit of worry because I knew it had to end with Pinklon on the floor and that was in the back of my mind. When the final bell rang and he was still standing, I knew I had lost. I also knew I was going to get blackballed after the fight, which did happen; Don cut off all ties with me. I knew I had the task of starting again so, after the fight, we just went off and celebrated a little bit. We were all aware of what Don was doing, so we just thought "What the hell?" and I had some beers and just forgot about it all for a while.

I knew I was out in the wilderness and, if I had let my heart rule my head at that moment, maybe I would have gone totally crazy. From my point of view, I was 27 years old and in the prime of my life. Up to then, my training had been pretty intense; I was usually in shape and the drugs hadn't got a hold of me at that point. I was just using them recreationally and cleaning myself up before training for the next fight. I am not the only fighter in the world who ever did that. Things are much tighter now, but that's the way it was. Then, suddenly, I was staring into the abyss. I wasn't going to get a chance to fight because I was totally cut off. Going from being the Heavyweight Champion of the World, and having money and a purpose, to having nothing was really tough, and I struggled with that. In my mind, I said to myself I had to find another way of making money and this is when I bought the grocery store, thinking it would hold me up, but I didn't bank on the drugs starting to take a hold of me.

I would be embarrassed if Tommy Wade could hear me now, because he kept us away from all of that. The time when I was away on a field-trip with the football team and they put a line of cocaine down there in front of me, I couldn't have been any more than 19 years old. I took a little bit and nothing happened and I just walked away. When I was first around Mark Stewart and all of those people is when I started doing lines of coke but, like I say, I really didn't know what those guys were up to; I just thought this was part of the lifestyle. Progressing in the sport, and meeting people, started me off in that direction, but I never did it in high school except for that one time, even though it was all around my neighbourhood.

I was still training here and there but, for about the first three weeks after the Pinklon fight, I was doing drugs constantly. I started doing crack whilst my family ran the store. They knew something was up but they didn't really know what I was doing. Then somebody introduced me to freebasing. I remember, the first time I did it, I was really scared. I felt really bad that I did it; my heart was pumping and I thought I was despicable and no good. I did it one time, and then the next time I did it was a couple of months later when something brought me back to it. I was upstairs doing it whilst my family were working downstairs. I would come downstairs, get some beers, and then I would go back up. I was depressed, and I was doing exactly what you are supposed to do if you get bumped off by Don; that is the way a lot of boxers went. I didn't know where my career was going. It gradually got worse. I had guys from the neighbourhood coming around and we were cooking up the freebase. I would put it in pure ammonia. You would sit it in there and then get a hot plate that had been on top of the stove; the hot plate burns the ammonia and you get a rock forming. When it gets hard, you scrape it up and then you smoke it. I was doing that for a long time – every time I cooked it up, I would mess it up – and there looked like there was only one way I was going to go with my life.

After a while, I couldn't hide it and, when people found out what I was doing, they were really shocked. I went to New York to see one of my friends and he saw how skinny I was and said: "Tim, are you messing with that stuff?" I told him the truth. He made me stay up in New York for a little while to get away from it and, when I came back home, I just woke up. I said to myself I had to find a way to get back to Don King for, at that moment, despite everything, that was the only place I could think of where I could get salvation. Okay, I was getting ripped off but, without the discipline of boxing, I was a mess. I needed it; I had to have the focus. I was stuck between the devil and the deep blue sea and I knew the motherfucker was going to keep on the same way because he was holding all the cards. We were like battery hens in cages, us boxers, and, at any time, Don could take another one of us out and chase us with his shotgun. If you kept quiet and just took the money that he was offering, you were okay and, at that point in time, I thought that was something I could do, something I had to do if I was going to carry on.

Even though I knew he was wrong, I had to find a plan to get back with Don. I called him from New York and I called him from Vegas, because I'd called managers and promoters and nobody would touch me. They all said "No" because Don still had me and they couldn't do anything for me. I was locked out, so my plan was to tell him that I was sorry and to really try to convince him that I was sincere. I wanted to make him believe that I was on his side. So I got Aaron Snowell to call him and to say I was sorry, and to set up a meeting. He said "Fuck you", the first time. Then Aaron called again and this time Don hung up the phone. I think it was the fourth or fifth time that things changed because Aaron went through Carl King and he convinced his father of how sorry I was. We set up a 'phone call and I spoke to Don and told him I was sorry; I told him I didn't mean all the stuff I said in the papers; and I told him I was wrong. I couldn't believe the words which were coming out of my mouth.

Even though I thought 100 per cent what he had done to me was wrong, I had to let him know that I had changed and that I was going to come back and be a flunky for him. After the very first conversation we had, nothing happened. Then Aaron called Carl again and he told us to come up and meet his dad because he had agreed for us all to talk. So, I went in and saw him. I told him again I was sorry and that I didn't know what had happened to me and that it wasn't going to happen again. I had to keep saying sorry to him for months. He told me I had to go to the newspapers and keep saying I was sorry to them, and I had to promote Don as a good guy for a long time. Even the journalists knew I was lying, but this was my plan to get me back with a shot at the title and, after a while, it began to work.

I had a lay-off of seven months between the fight against Pinklon and my next opponent in March 1985, Mark Willis, who Don said would be easy. There was a continuing campaign for me to say how sorry I was and I was still doing it leading up to the fight. I was told the fight would be easy to get me back into things, and that I would knock him out without any problems. I trained, but not like I should have, and the drug use had definitely affected me. We flew into LA for the fight at the Forum in Inglewood and we had the same crew as a lot of good fighters on the card. Don flew all of them in. As soon as I got into the airport, the guy who picked us up said: "Hey Tim, are you in shape? The guy you're fighting is going to give you a fight; he's tough." I knew I wasn't in the best shape, but I thought I was getting an easy opponent who I could KO. We got to the hotel and the people there were asking me the same thing, and they told me Mark could punch. So what I did was start running. This was five or six days before the fight. Then I realized that, if I hit the training hard, I would be tired. So I ran for one day and then I rested. I knew I would have to take my chance.

When we got into the ring, I looked at him and I saw that he was solid and muscular. The first round went okay and then – bam! – I suddenly realized he could punch. I dropped him in the second round, but every round after that, he kicked my ass; he hit me hard; he beat me up. I was losing the fight; there was blood in my mouth. I went back to my corner and I was told I was going to get beaten so I dug in deep and I knocked him out in the ninth round. It was a hell of a fight. I was so tired, but it was then I realised that your mind is stronger than your body. After the fight, I went out to the bathroom and I urinated blood. My eyes were swollen; he did a really good job of hurting me. It was the worst fight of my career because I went past the limit my body could take. I kept saying to myself: "This bastard set me up." I flew home and still I had to keep apologising; I had to tell the media that Don King was the greatest man in the world, and that I was sorry for what I had said about him. I had won the fight but I had learned the hard way about what happens if you run your mouth.

The average person in the street would be thinking I was apologising because I had made a mistake, but everybody in boxing knew what was really happening. After I paid everybody, I think I got about $20,000 for the Mark Willis fight but I was on my way back up, and I was lined up to fight James Broad in Buffalo 35 days later. James was big and he was arrogant and the fight was for the North American Boxing Federation Championship. We went up into the woods to the Buffalo training camp and I chopped a lot of wood. There was a lot of big names at the camp. There was David Bey, Mitch Green, Greg Page, Michael "Dynamite" Dukes, Azumah Nelson, all training hard. James Broad was a lot bigger than me and I knew a lot of people didn't like him and it would be a good opportunity for me to build up my profile. I was a good guy. Okay, I did a little bit of drugs, but I wouldn't say I really had a habit apart from when I got depressed after the Pinklon fight. I was still using recreationally; if the fight was two months away, I would lay off the drugs, say, a month before, and then maybe when it was over, I would do a little bit more. But, generally, people liked me and didn't like James and they wanted to see me kick his ass.

This is around the time Don King was promoting the Jacksons' Victory Tour, which was the only time all six of the children performed together. Don put $3m into the tour and the album but Michael Jackson was unhappy with the controversial ticket-lottery system that had been set up, and he ended up donating all of his earnings to charity and effectively split away from the rest of the family. When Don was trying to get Michael to sign up for the tour, I almost blew it for him because of everything I was saying in the papers. I used to talk a lot with Jermaine Jackson because he watched a lot of fights. He came up to me when I was at the Dorchester Hotel in London and he asked me what was wrong and why I'd been saying all of this stuff to the newspapers. He was wondering if Don was taking my money, and I just smiled at him and said "Yes", but not to tell anybody, and I think he may have gone and told his family.

It took Michael Jackson another six months before he signed up for the tour. I know he didn't need the money because things were still going crazy with the Thriller album, and I guess he didn't trust Don, either. I think, through all of us guys complaining, the word probably got back to Michael and I know he did the tour reluctantly. Joe, LaToya and Janet Jackson were at the James Broad fight and I remember walking out to the ring and being a little nervous because he was a big dude. When the bell rang, I was straight in, hitting him hard, and then, in the second round, I sparked him right out. I kept on hitting him with about 15 head shots and he was totally gone, with only the ropes holding him up. He went down and I could see Todd Bridges, who played Willis Jackson from Diff'rent Strokes, in the crowd, going crazy as James hit the canvas. I think his ear was busted and his trunks even ripped as he crashed to the ground, where Janet Jackson was left staring at his butt.

Chapter Twelve

On the way...to Rehab

I THINK I got about 25 grand for the James Broad fight, and I went home and a started doing drugs straightaway, although I didn't stay home that long. One of the stipulations when I got back with Don was that I couldn't stay and I had to go back to the camp where the meter was running; you couldn't even enjoy being with your family. My son, Tim junior, who I brought into the ring with me after the fight, was only six months old and, after seven days at home, I had to go back to camp. One of the reasons for this was because Don could keep running up the tab for his taxes. The guy didn't miss a trick. He had accountants on his pay-roll, but I had a better accountant in Steve Ratner.

I fought James "Bonecrusher" Smith on April 15, 1985, and we were chopping a lot of wood for this guy because he was big and strong, and he was very clever; he was the first Heavyweight Champion of the World to have a college degree. He could also punch. He was born in North Carolina and he turned professional late on, in 1981, when he was 28 years old. I knew he had lost a couple of fights so I believed I could beat him and keep hold of the NABF. So we went to the camp and I really had to train because I knew he was strong and I was still on my way back up. I fought again at the Riviera in Vegas – they had a deal with Don and we would always go there and train in their gyms a little bit early, maybe three weeks or a month before the fight.

You must understand that, every time I'm going into the ring now, I know I'm going to get ripped off. I was probably going to walk away with $10,000 or so a fight by the time I paid everything, but I didn't really know exactly how much I would get and that was always on my mind. The Internal Revenue Service came in and took everybody's money before that and I think they were surprised because they were expecting all of the top boxers to be getting more money than they were picking up, so they had to look into it all. I didn't even ask Don how much I was getting anymore, but Carl King would whisper to me "Hey, I think you're getting this amount of money" and that is all I had to go by. So, I went into the Bonecrusher fight (and I think I may have picked up $25,000, when it should have been $300,000, maybe $400,000) and I won every round. I almost knocked him out in three of the rounds, and I felt really good for that fight. I was in the kind of condition I was in when I fought Larry Holmes. In all of those fights in between, I didn't feel as good as I felt for the Bonecrusher fight, and also for the fight against Tony Tubbs. I was in really good shape.

I beat Bonecrusher – I got the unanimous decision – and I was going to get a couple months off until my next fight. I was still drinking, and doing all of this other stuff, after the fights, but I knew I was on the way back up. In my personal life, I had my new baby son Tim, but I was cheating on his mother Tammy, who I had got with after the fight against Larry, and I had a daughter called Indya behind her back with Tracie. I did my best to be a father but, like I said, I really didn't have a role-model; all I had was Tommy, and my uncle, Jake Loman, when I was growing up. It was tough being away at camp a lot of the time. I look back and wish somebody had given me that kick up the butt I so desperately needed back then to get me off of the drugs and get me back in line, and I think I would have had a lot more stability if I was in a good, solid, loving relationship. I don't blame Tammy for leaving; she'd had enough. As I've said, Linda was too good for me and she really didn't have a chance when the boxing took off just as we were getting started; it was a shame. I know I made a big mess. I didn't tell Tracie the truth, either. When I did, it was already too late.

    I guess my life has always been all over the place. I've travelled all across the world, and I've hung out with many different types of people. Some of them were bad, or they were hangers-on, and I don't think I was always smart enough to find out who was who. I trusted people because I wanted to believe in the good side of human nature, and when you have nothing and nobody, maybe it is easier to distinguish the good people – they are the ones who come and help you out when you have nothing to give back in return. So many people would say "Sure, Tim", telling me it wasn't a problem, they could do that, or they could fix this, but a lot of them wanted something in return. I always had my inner circle of family and close friends, of course, but sometimes I wanted to believe somebody was as nice and genuine as they come across, although they may have been hiding their true intentions. Look how I've already described Don King. I said that I like him as a person; I saw him as a jolly old guy who was ripping people off. So it shows you that I still wanted to believe in the good in people, despite what some of them have done to me.

Things were good with Tammy for a while but eventually it got heavy and she got involved with another guy, too. I remember I was really crazy. I was driving down the street with my brother and we had guns on us; I was going to shoot the guy's tyres out. That's how mad I was at that time. All hell broke loose when we split; I had everything going on with Don, and my mind was all over the place. I did some bad things I'm not proud of, but it ended up with us chasing Tammy and her new boyfriend down the street and we caught them. I was really hurt because we were together and then she left, but I don't think I would have shot her boyfriend; I don't think I had that in me unless my family or someone was in danger of their lives. Even though I had all this crack cocaine and other shit floating around in my system, I just felt really hurt, and I guess I didn't see it from a calmer point of view because my mind was not clear. I had cheated on Linda, and I did the same with Tammy. Being who I was, and being away from home so much, of course there were beautiful ladies around me and sometimes the temptation got too much. I take responsibility for my own actions, of course I do, and I will always have to live with the bad decisions I made.

Like I say, I was going to shoot this guy's tyres out but my brother grabbed my hand at the last minute and swung the car around. We almost crashed into a pole and, by the time I lifted my head up, the car was gone. He saved my life. I thought I saw the car go one way, but he told me it went in another direction, so we didn't find them. What I did to get satisfaction was drive all the way down to South Philly, to Tammy's sister's house, and we shot her car windows out. That's how crazy I was at that time, and there weren't a lot of people who were going to get in my way. My brother knew I was emotional, so he took the guns from me and he shot the rest of the windows out, then we drove back home. I look back on all of this now after so many years and I wonder exactly what my thought-processes were. I could have lost it all just as I was rebuilding it, but I let my anger get the better of me.

After the Bonecrusher fight, the partying started again. I was on the road, but I had surrounded myself with a lot of people who just wanted to cash in on my name; they didn't really care about Tim Witherspoon, but why should they? I guess I didn't really care about myself for a little while, with everything I was doing. There was no real guidance. The people who helped me in my childhood were either old, or living back in Philly, and I was travelling all over. I was drinking cough syrup around this time too, cocktails. There were cough syrups and pills which contained codeine, and there were others which contained morphine; you mix them both together and they call it "pancakes and syrup." All through the court proceedings with Don, I was drinking it. Every morning, I was falling asleep during the meetings with the lawyers and they were nudging me to wake me up.

My next fight was against Larry Beilfuss, down in Miami, and it was a real calamity. Larry looked about 60 years old, and it was one of the times in my life I did not feel like fighting and putting the gloves down. I wasn't in that good a shape because I knew this was a fight just for the statistics, to get me another KO, but I thought they would have found me an opponent who at least stood a chance. I told Don I couldn't fight him because I would kill him; he said: "Just knock-him out, beat his ass. I've put some money in front of you so do what I say." But I couldn't do it. Larry was old and defenceless. So I said to myself: "I'm going to do my best to make sure this guy does not get hurt." When we got in the ring, he took his robe off, and I could see all of this flab hanging down. He was really big but I could have knocked him out with one hand tied behind my back, that's how shameful I felt. Don King told me to get him out of there, so what I did was slap him. I didn't have my fist balled up inside the glove; I just slapped him on the head. And he went down. I couldn't believe it. I was acting like I was hitting him, but nobody knew what I was doing. I slapped him again and he went down, but got back up; I slapped him again and, when he fell, they stopped it. It was the easiest fight of my life. I kept saying to him "I'm sorry" after the fight; it was just a shame they put him in front of me.

I flew to Birmingham NEC for my next bout in October 1985. I fought on the undercard of the Azumah Nelson-Pat Cowdell WBC featherweight title fight, against a fighter called Sammy Scaff. He was a much more aggressive opponent, but I knew he was in there to lose; it was just another statistical fight for my record. He was hard and durable and I just said to him: "Look man, I'm in shape. If you try to fight me, you are going to get hurt." He was a big guy, though, and I said to him that nobody was expecting me to lose and that he should try not to get hurt but he still tried to fight me. I stopped him in the fourth with a TKO; he went down and I think he got up, but they called it off. It was a big night in England and Pat Cowdell got knocked out by Azumah. We were in the ring and people started throwing stuff and shouting; then Carl King started taunting them and that started a riot. When we all got out of the ring, our group got attacked so me and Sammy stuck together and nobody attacked me for some reason. Everybody was fighting, and people were hitting the deck and I'm trying to help them up, but nobody attacked me. Sammy's corner man got a broken cheek bone; it was a really big fight. We tried to regroup and Carl King was shouting "Let's go back and fight them" but I knew it wasn't a good idea so we didn't do it. I said to him: "Let's just sit back, I know the fans have tried to kill us but we've won the fight, so let's leave it alone."

On December 8, 1985, I signed a contract with Don to fight Tony "TNT" Tubbs in Georgia for the WBA Heavyweight Championship of the World. The contract stated that the purse was to be $500,000 and Don was to charge me the usual training fees for at least 14 days before the fight. They were also to provide me with five airline tickets, five hotel rooms, and three meals a day for five people for 14 days. I won the decision after 15 rounds to become the Heavyweight Champion of the World once again on January 17, 1986. Up to that point, Tubbs was undefeated – he had had 22 wins and 15 knockouts – whereas I'd lost two from 25, with 16 KOs. We went at it all fight, and even in the last round we were both raining in shots, mostly to each other's body. I did just have the edge, though, and I had a little bit more left in the tank than Tubbs, but he was a tough opponent. I just went for it for the last 30 seconds or so, raining punches in at his head, some of which did not connect. There were policemen all around the ring to stop an invasion and, when the last bell rang, the referee had to pull us apart. We both raised our hands in victory but, if you look at the way we both did it, you can see that Tubbs was in trouble, whereas I went dancing over to my corner. When everybody was in the ring, me and Tony hugged and then we went back to our corners to wait for the verdict. When I heard I had taken the title from him, I raised my hands in the air and they lifted me up on to their shoulders. I was only the third man in history to lift the title twice. From the bottom, I had come right back and it was to be my own foolishness which would set me back this time.

After the Tony Tubbs fight, I tested positive for marijuana. On my birthday, somebody had been passing the joint around and I only took about five or six drags but it showed up in my body. There wasn't any real testing going on at the time, mostly for championship fights, but the fight was in Georgia where nobody can be bought and I didn't know that. Down there, it was run by a bible-punching white-man, and nobody could bribe or threaten him, except God. Everybody went to church; the place was straight down the line. When it happened, Don said to me "Why the fuck are you smoking weed?" and I had to go into rehab. It was crazy. Everybody who was in that class had big drug problems and I attended for three months, which I had to do or else I would be in breach of my conditions, and I was only just getting myself together. I have read about sportsmen and performers for who the buzz they feel when they are performing doesn't come around in normal life. That is why a lot of them use drugs and drink and stuff. I suppose there was some of that in me, too, but I did have a lot of different things weighing down on me, and I was right in the middle of it all. It wasn't like I could see a light at the end of the tunnel and, after the drugs thing, I thought I could be going down the tubes once again. I don't know how much of an influence Don had on the outcome but I got away with it relatively cheaply, so I was definitely lucky in some respects.

After camp, I would get driven down to rehab; I would sit in a group and everybody would tell their story. There was this dishevelled crackhead who told us all how he got caught up in it. Then they moved on to a guy who looked like he needed feeding up; he was dirty and he had been using heroin all the time. Then they moved on to me. I was sat there wearing nice clothes and jewellery and, when they asked me, I said: "My name is Tim Witherspoon. I'm the Heavyweight Champion of the World, and all I did was smoke a joint." The other guys said to me I could be there because I was the champ, but they also said they needed the help more than me, and I guess they were right. I didn't get banned, though; they made me pay a fine and I was told I would have my licence suspended if I tested positive again. This was when I first starting thinking about the effects of the drugs for the very first time. I was in there with the drug education people and I learned a lot of stuff I didn't know about before.

In April 1986, before I fought Frank Bruno, Tony Tubbs and I signed an agreement for a rematch to take place in New York City in December for the WBA title. We were friends; we had been at Ali's camp when we were both starting out and we turned pro around the same time. In the contract, it said I was to receive $250,000 for my fee, with Don providing his usual costly services. This time, I was given ten of everything – airplane tickets, hotel rooms and meals –and ringside seats for all of my people, and we were all ready for the training. Everything was going ahead, but Don scratched out Tubbs' name and put Bonecrusher Smith in there instead, and I wasn't interested in fighting him again. They also increased my training expenses, and both Don and Carl signed the contract acknowledging those changes. There was no signature from me because I didn't even know the changes had been made. All of this stuff comes straight from the reports the solicitor showed the court.

Chapter Thirteen

Frank Bruno

I WAS drug-tested in early January 1986. Like I said, I smoked half a joint at birthday party, not realizing I was going to get tested. We were having a meal, I was still recovering from the fight against Tony Tubbs, and I just did it. It wasn't any kind of performance-enhancing substance; it was just marijuana, straight off of the bush and into a cigarette, and boy didn't it make some waves for me? I've seen lots of people really drunk doing lots of crazy shit; I've seen crackheads going out of their minds when they can't get a hit; I had my flirtation with all of that shit – it had taken over my life for a time, and I was still meddling with it, in and out. When I tested positive, I had none of that in my system, just a little bit of cannabis, and that is what they got me on.

I went back to training but I wasn't thinking too much about the test at the time, despite the fact that I knew I was going to be in trouble. I was thinking about something else I had done, something more important to me, something now at risk of being taken away. I was, as I've already mentioned, only the third man in history to regain the championship title and it really meant a lot to me. I felt like Ali, but I wasn't treated like he was when he was the champ. I knew, even though I was the number one, I was only going to be left with around $8,000. The IRS did come in and take some of the money but, after deductions, that is all that I had to show for winning the Heavyweight Championship of the World. I think I even ended up borrowing money after that fight, when really I should been taking home purses in the hundreds of thousands. I have some paperwork from the court case against Don showing some of those purses. There was one where I received just over $40,000 from a $250,000 dollar purse, with deductions of $125,000 paid to my "manager" Carl King. It wasn't like I was being extravagant with millions, or hundreds of thousands, of dollars. If I was being paid properly, I would have been alright.

Don was angry with me over the drug test for a while because the next fight he was setting up for me was a multi-million dollar fight and I'd set things back. I only realized he had something big planned afterwards, and this is why he did all of these things like putting me in rehab, but they let me keep the belt because they had to make sure the fight against Frank Bruno went through, and the Georgia Boxing Commission were not bothered about me fighting in England. The bout would have probably taken place earlier if it wasn't for what I did, but I ended up stepping out in front of 40,000 people at Wembley Stadium in London in July 1986 for a fight I wasn't sure I could win at first. I knew Bonecrusher had beaten Bruno, but the media interest was amazing; it was like the whole of England was behind him and that made me wonder whether or not I could win.

I was training hard, but I was thinking it was just another fight, that I was going to go over to London and knock him out. I had been in England for the Sammy Scaff fight but I'd never really thought about the country and the people, so I was surprised. We flew over with a whole bunch of guys and, when we landed, I really didn't know the enormity of the occasion. They had a group of security men escorting us along to our buses and I suddenly had a whole bunch of beautiful woman hanging off of me as we went into the airport. The Press were there and they were taking pictures and I'm still not really realizing it was going to be the biggest fight of my life. I was just having fun, and then we got in the cars and we were driving around and our plans changed. Don said "Wait a minute, were going to go out to the countryside to train" and we ended up in Basildon because he didn't want us staying over the top of a pub where they would be sending girls up and trying to get me drunk. So he just moved the camp and we started training at the Basildon Leisure Centre. The fight was promoted by Mickey Duff's company "Terrible Twosome" who allocated purses of $1.7m to me, and a million for Bruno, and they paid the money straight to Don.

I felt really bad and I knew something was wrong when they sent everybody home from my entourage and left me and my Tammy behind in the hotel. They changed our flights; they didn't give us any money; and we stayed in Basildon whilst everyone else left. We just walked about the place, wondering what was happening, and what we should do. If Don had told me I had only got $95,000 whilst everyone was there, he knew there would have been trouble because I had my brothers there and people would have been getting hurt. I guess he was fearing some kind of repercussions but that could have all been avoided if he had paid me what I was worth. Then again, people were worthless to him, and us boxers were just pieces of shit for him to clamber over.

Sending everybody home was a really smart move because Don knew I had to pay everybody. We flew home later on and I called him. His daughter Debbie answered the 'phone and I said: "Debbie how much have I got? Are you ready to send my cheque?" She said I had $95,000 and I started cursing and going crazy. No-one really told me before what I was getting; it should have been at least $1.7 million, but that was not the case. I was still hoping for a million; I wouldn't have asked about the rest. I said to her there must be some kind of a mistake because I was supposed to get half a million. She told me I needed to talk to her father because I only had $95,000. When he called me later, he said "Timmy, you've got a nickel" meaning $500,000, before he went on about the deductions. Carl King took $250,000 and another $75,000 was for income tax. WBC took $25,000 for their fine; the WBA took $15,000; and there was another charge of $45,000 for miscellaneous expenses. From the fight against Bruno, I received just $95,000, plus a $25,000 bonus from Don. I negotiated the $25,000 bonus with Don myself because he was only going to pay me the flat money.

I started cursing and said "This is crazy, man" but he said that was the way it was, and I hung the 'phone up on him. I later found out that the deductions, the miscellaneous fees taken out of my money, were expenses for all of the officials and different people he flew into London for the fight. There was nothing I could do at the time, but I couldn't just take it on the chin again. After the Bruno fight, I got started on the drugs once again. It wasn't like it was taking over my life, but it was a form of relaxation to get away from all the bad stuff that was happening around me. I could not believe the amount of money I was being paid. It felt like I was whoring myself out for the championship of the world.

I know other people have felt this way about Don, and I remembered Ali's words – he knew I was going to get ripped off. There was a time in the early 1980s when somebody attacked Don physically, but that was not something I planned to do. I didn't feel that way, but I know there were people on my side who were ready to step in if he tried to attack me. What angered me was the way he could be so nice to your face. I have already said I liked the guy, the jovial old man taking everybody's money with a smile and a line of bullshit. When I came back on board, I proved myself to him. I had even grovelled at his feet to get back into his good books. The fight against Bruno would have given me a certain amount of independence and, financially, I could have got myself into good shape. This was how it was with Don; he would give you a little bit of freedom, but he was always the puppet-master. He would give a fighter that had won the championship a certain amount of liberties, but he was shrewd enough to keep us all on the end of his strings.

When my court case against Don got underway, I knew my life was under threat. There had been people telling me this directly, telling me I had to shut up and take what I had been given and just move on with my life. Any time I was in public, there were people around who were protecting me, and they had guns in their coats. This was in no way what I wanted. I'm not a gangster; I'm a sportsman. I saw all of this going on in the hood when I was growing up but I was never involved. I was just mad, just as the people around me were, too. I just wanted my money; I wanted to be paid fairly for the fight. It should have been the kind of money a man should get when he fights for or defends the Heavyweight Championship of the World.

So, after the Bruno fight, we stayed for a couple of days with friends in England. I was walking around without any money after successfully defending the title. In my mind, I was wondering what was going on because I knew Don was trying to pull something. Back home, when I found out about the money, I was really messed up, and I said "That is it, I am going to need to find a way to get away from him." I knew I couldn't take such a big loss and I said to my lawyers that we would have to look into suing him, so we did. Everybody thought I was lying when I told them how much I'd got from the fight. Even my brothers said "No way, that cannot be true", but then I showed them the receipt. I gave everybody who was working for me a fair amount and I had about $60,000 left after everything had been paid. I was telling everyone that Don was crazy because, if he had given me a decent amount of money, then I wouldn't have taken him to court. That is how bad the situation was - I was willing to get ripped off for the rest of my money.

You have to remember that, every time we went into the ring, we were risking our lives. I know people look up to boxers as some kind of supermen and, in a way, we were. We were all still men though, flesh and blood bags that were able to bleed and break if hit hard enough, and there are many who are suffering from the effects of those days in the ring today. Take a look at some of the boxers who were under Don – there are high-profile fighters like Mike Tyson, but there are other fighters still living and still breathing and they are struggling because they did not get the fortunes they should have got. You have to ask yourself what it was all for. People were risking their lives just for that belt. The American dream says a man or a woman can reach the very top from the bottom and become a champion, a President, a businessman, or a rock star. You are one of the privileged few if you scale the summit and become number one, and you would expect to be paid your worth. Don had it all wrong. He was a brilliant promoter but, if he had been fair, he would have gone down in history as one of the greatest of all time. Instead, he ripped off and destroyed some of the biggest stars of the 20th century.

When all of the dust settled, after the years I had in the wilderness, all of the stresses and strains of the court case and life in general, I would come out of it with $1.2m. However, I do not see this as winning – this money was paid to keep things from going to court. Whilst working for Don, I spent my time promoting him, not me, the boxer. I was in a situation where I was saying to myself: "This guy could have been so great; he could have been so well respected if he could just stop, and start treating people right." There is something in his blood that just made him keep on going and doing whatever he wanted to do, to hell with other people.

Back home, everyone was congratulating me everywhere I went, telling me I had done well against Bruno, and retained my title and kept my dream intact; I just had a bitter taste in my mouth. I had it in my mind to keep going as the champ, it was what I had always wanted, but I should have felt better than I did, and I should have been financially secure. Not just from the Bruno fight, but from the other fights, going all the way back to Larry Holmes. I had always wanted to fight in front of a really big crowd and the atmosphere at Wembley that evening was electric. Coming back victorious after beating a British icon in his own backyard, and that feeling of total elation, was one of the highlights of my career. As the story seems to go with me, after the good, there always seems to be a little bit of bad. Some of it I could have controlled myself, but other things just escalated from my situation. There wasn't anybody I really trusted who was not being paid by Don. Even Slim, who had taught me everything, was working for Don and he had to look out for himself. I was still the champ, but I knew what was going to happen now. I had to do it. It had gone too far now.

When I was training in Basildon, people were there and I was signing autographs, signing gloves and pictures, as it was getting closer to the fight. After I finished sparring one day, I went to the hotel and there were about 20 black guys waiting for me, Jamaicans who had come up from Brixton to see me. They told me I was looking in good shape, and I said I was going up to my room and they followed me up there. So I opened the door and I let them come in. I had security with me but it wasn't like they were any kind of threat; they were good guys. All they wanted was to get some pictures signed and to have a little bit of time, and I had no problem with that at all. Then they were telling me to kick Bruno's ass and I said to them that I thought he was one of their brothers because they were all black and they were from the same town. They told me that they felt Frank did not go and help the blacks out, that he just stayed around the whites all the time, and they did not want him to win. I said to myself: "Maybe I really can do this." It gave me another little bit of confidence; it was then that I realized there were more than a few people who wanted me to win. I knew this vibe must also have been there in Frank's head, which was another thing we had against him. In my mind, it put the icing on the cake and I just wanted to get started.

When we were at the weigh-in for the fight, I remember I managed to catch Bruno. I told him that he had not seen the things I had; he had not seen violence or anybody get shot; he had never seen anybody dead; and I had seen all of these things. Okay, I've seen some bad stuff – I even saw that guy get killed in the gang fight –but I made out that I was more involved than I actually was. Then I looked at him in his eyes and he got a little bit scared and I said to myself: "Oh, I got to him!" So I went back and told everybody that I had scared him a little bit. He had put his head to one side and he looked down at me when I made that statement, and I knew I had him. Another thing – his hands were really big and they were trying to get him to use bigger gloves but my trainer Slim said "No", he was going to wear the same gloves I was wearing, and that he couldn't have a special pair made for him. All of these things played on Bruno's mind a little bit – he wasn't wearing the right gloves; he was unsure of what kind of a person I was – and it just gave me that slight advantage a boxer sometimes needs, especially against an opponent like Frank Bruno, who is big and strong.

We travelled up from Basildon and checked in at the arena. When we were all in the dressing-room, everybody was a little bit nervous, but I was up there, joking and messing around. I looked around the room as I got ready to go and I saw the nerves in everyone's faces; I was nervous, too, but I was playing around to try and hide it. This is when a good trainer is needed, and Slim came into the dressing-room and, as I started to tie my boots, he just started to talk to me. He told me I was great and I just started to gain confidence. Then the music started going and I stood up and looked him straight in the eyes. I smiled at him and I said I was ready to go into battle; then we started walking out towards the ring and it was all over. As we headed towards the ring, there were all of these people – it was unbelievable. They were all singing: "Bruno! Bruno! Bruno!" I had my hands up all the way to the ring; they let me in, and it was the most beautiful feeling I ever felt in my life. Here I was, defending my title, with all of these people screaming against me, and Frank Bruno was in there, waiting. As soon as I got in, I walked straight into the centre, and he walked in and we were just stood there, staring at each other. The atmosphere was electric. It was just us, alone in the ring, like we were the only ones in the universe. You cannot dream of this moment unless you have experienced it for yourself. I had been in very big fights, but I had never felt like this before. When I first got into boxing and I dreamt about fighting for the Heavyweight Championship of the World (remember, I never had an idea that I would ever do it) what I dreamt was the same as I felt at that moment. I felt like Marciano, Sonny Liston, and Muhammad Ali all rolled into one. Finally, Tim Witherspoon had arrived and this was my moment.

Chapter Fourteen

Throwing the Title

IT was an honor having Muhammad Ali spar with me for a couple of my fights. He was just returning the favour, I guess, but we were friends. He liked me, and this is where the misconception comes from that he gave me the "Terrible Tim" nickname. I saw him a few years back in Manchester but he didn't really recognise me. He looked at me and there was a glimmer of something passing across his face; with the Parkinson's and everything, I think it was just a little bit too much for him. For the Bruno fight, he wanted to support me, so Don flew him over to London, I guess. I've seen pictures of us standing side by side in the camp dinner-queue with plates in our hands, joking around. I don't know who took the pictures, with him telling me that I was going to get ripped off by Don, but that is what he told me. However, there was really nothing I could do about it. I felt like I was being choked and, the further along I went, the less air I was breathing.

Straight after the Bruno fight, I was doing an interview but I noticed that the atmosphere had changed and I saw some people starting to throw stuff and a little bit of trouble was starting. I looked around for Don, but he had disappeared. I don't know how he got out of there, but we were all left to defend ourselves. We had about 20 big bodyguards around us but it was still a very worrying time. Before we started walking, one of the security men said to us that, if we were to fall, then we were at risk of being killed, so we had to keep moving and keep our feet high. We were going at the same speed as the security because we did not want to be trampled to death. We started heading towards the dressing-rooms while chairs, coins, and all kinds of stuff started flying towards us. They were hitting us, and this is when I knew it was serious.

I saw a person get thrown over the top of the crowd as we were passing by. I also saw a police officer take his helmet off and he hit this guy right in the face, and I saw all of the blood everywhere. I knew we were in a really serious situation and I was worried about my partner Tammy, who is just over 5ft. She was underneath me and I was protecting her and I told her to keep moving. We were pushing stuff out of the way and we managed to get into the corridor and inside the dressing-room and they sealed it off and held the people back. Then Ali came in and nobody was going to mess with him; he can walk into any kind of crowd and they will part for him, and this is what happened. It was like Moses parting the Red Sea. We were all inside the dressing-room and we could hear people banging at the door, trying to kick it in. It was a massive door and it was just about to be broken down with a couple of hundred people outside, trying to get in. Then Ali said "Step back" and he shouted

"Open the door" and the security said "No way." He said it again and they did it and, as soon as the crowd saw Muhammad Ali, everybody stopped. He turned all of those people around and he told them to go. Then they locked the door. That just shows you the power that he has; it was a beautiful moment.

If you remember, Tony Tubbs was scheduled for a rematch with me to contest the championship and it was going to take place in December 1986. Then they told me he hurt his shoulder in training. I don't know if they paid him or whatever, but they switched the fighter and I was then told I would be fighting Bonecrusher Smith for a second time. Even though I didn't want to do this, I was told I had to. They sat me in a room and I was told to do it or I would get hurt, and this is when all those high-ranking officials and associates came in and pressured me. I had beaten Bonecrusher fair and square before, so the prospect of a rematch did not fill me with happiness. Later, when I spoke to him, he said: "Man, I thought something was up, I was told to go at you and that is what I did." I had made sure that the three-knockdown rule was in place and I took full advantage and admit to throwing the fight. By doing it, I had lost the thing I wanted most of all – that world belt – and I suppose you can say it makes a mockery of such a coveted title as the Heavyweight Championship of the World. I know people are going to be sad and annoyed with such a revelation, but believe me when I say my mental health was at risk if I did not get away from Don King.

The Bonecrusher fight ended up taking place on December 12, 1986, at Madison Square Garden. We had been hatching a plan to get away from Don and now I knew what I was going to do. I didn't train as hard as I could have done and I took a little bit of cocaine maybe three or four days before the fight. Bonecrusher knocked me down three times in the first round, and that was the only the time that happened in my career, even at the end when I was in my mid-40s. If you watch the fight, you will notice that Don King had the new WBC champion Mike Tyson ringside that night, and the winner was to go on a fight him. If you watch me, I look nervous, but I just needed to get away from Don and start again. I sometimes wonder what would have happened if I had fought Mike. I know I had the power to stop him if I hit him but I would have needed to have been in the best condition of my life.

I was carrying about 12lb more than I did when I first fought Bonecrusher but, as I said, I had not trained properly. He came right at me and attacked from the start and I didn't really throw anything back at him. He had me against the ropes; I managed to get a right in, but I was defending myself, ducking and bobbing. Then, in the corner, I unloaded with a big right and he went to the ground. He got straight back up and carried on throwing punches as I defended my head. Then he hit me with a right and I fell to my knee. A few seconds later, he came in once more and hit me and I hit the deck, before taking a standing eight count. The referee let the fight continue and Bonecrusher hit me around the head again. I did not hit back. When I hit the canvas for third time, I knew it was all over.

Before the fight, the commentators were talking about my weight and they were right about my condition. They were calling it a massive loss for me but, in truth, I was now free because I knew Don would tear up my contract when he saw what I had done. I was supposed to get $300,000, with $100,000 for training expenses. Don was managing both myself and Bonecrusher, which is not allowed. In the paperwork I have from my lawyers from the case against him, they concluded that I was forced to defend my WBC title, which is the truth. I don't think I signed anything, but they wanted me to fight Bonecrusher, and line us up against Tyson because their goal was to make him the youngest ever champion. We were all sitting down in Don's camp and I knew that he didn't give a fuck about any of us boxers. His eyes were only for Mike, and he was telling us "You'd better get in good shape because there is this young kid and he is strong" and that was the first time I heard of him. We knew Don was going to put us up against him and I was thinking "Who is this guy?" and then I saw him on TV fighting all kinds of opponents, bums most of them, and he was knocking everybody out. My mind was more occupied with being ripped off, but I saw Don slipping away from all of us boxers towards Mike.

The lawyers also said that the signatures on the contract to fight Bonecrusher were most probably forged, but I was happy because I could see a light at the end of the tunnel. As a matter of fact, I went to see my lawyer Dennis Richards right before the fight. We were down in Florida because Don sent us from the New York area as he thought all the lawyers were up there, but he didn't really know all the powerful people were down in Florida, and in Philly. From that fight, I also had the unlucky honour of being the only heavyweight champion to lose at Madison Square Garden. I know that I changed after the Bruno fight.

A guy called Art Pelullo helped me out a lot, and he gave

me the chance to start again. I had a couple of fights under him but, unfortunately, it didn't work out for us. There was a very intelligent Jewish guy called Dennis Rappaport who used to manage Gerry Cooney and he took an interest in me. Remember, after the Pinklon Thomas fight, nobody wanted to touch me; promoters steered clear because Don had a lot of friends. There were some very powerful businessman behind me after I finished with Don, and some of them also knew the commissioner so they ensured that no bad stuff went on for us. I felt like a great depression was gradually lifting off of me. I did have some scary moments –I will admit to that – and there was more than one time that I was in fear for the safety of myself, my children, and Tammy, so I ended up moving them west and out of Philly. My cousin Murad and his Muslim brothers were still watching out for me, but I remember there were guns everywhere: in the car; in cupboards in the house; and I also carried one for a time.

My future was uncertain but I was praying we would all come out of this alright, and I'd get the money I was owed. I was finally free and promoters wanted to talk to me again. I had the status and the reputation to continue and I was still a year away from my 30th birthday so I still had time to come back again. In the end, it all became too much for Tammy and that is why she left me. We had three young children together (Tim Junior, Ayanna and Mecca) and she got tired of people coming around; and all of us, including Tammy, were partying too much. I began to do this more often when the case against Don got underway, partly for protection, but also because I wanted to get high. I admit I put Tammy through a lot of pain and, of course, there was my daughter Indya who came from my affair with Tracie. They ended up moving in with me, and Indya even went to school with Tim Junior. We only lasted about five months and we did have some good times along the way, but I guess my lifestyle would have been too intense for any woman at that point in time.

Slim was one of the main players behind me suing Don King, although my manager Tom Moran wanted it to happen, too; he could always sniff a buck. Slim was in with Art Pelullo, and they got a gym on 25th Street in South Philly. It was big and beautiful and everybody went there, and we were special people because we knew Art. It took me another eight month to get my next fight, against Mark Willis, in August 1987, at the Resorts International in Atlantic City. By then, I was being represented by Dennis Rappaport. I got a hundred grand to fight for him, and then another hundred grand when the contract ran out. The fight ended with Willis getting TKO'd in the first round; if you remember, I had fought him before and he had given me a hard time, so I made sure I was ready this time.

Two months after that, I was in action once again at the Resorts International. "Mighty" Mike Williams was my opponent and I got the decision. I was getting in shape and we were going to back up the ladder again to try and get a shot at the title. He was strong, and in good condition; he was also up and coming, but I got the better of him in a hard fight. I convincingly beat him and I hurt him a couple of times, but I came off okay and I was still feeling good. I now had four months before the fight in London against Mexican champion Mauricio Villegas, which happened at the York Hall in Bethnal Green in February 1988, and I won by TKO in the ninth round. The fight was promoted by Frank Maloney and Ambrose Mendy, and I heard there was some betting activity going on around this fight. I also knew that my blood was dirty – I had been smoking marijuana – and when I heard news that I was going to be tested, I snuck out of the back door of York Hall to where the cars were waiting. Later on, they tried to get me in the hotel and Tom Moran gave the official the story that I had been celebrating and drinking and I was not in a fit state to do the test.

I didn't get into the ring for a professional fight for 11 months after that. This time, I faced Larry Alexander at Bally's in Vegas, which is a well-known hang-out for mobsters. Larry was big and strong but he had been beaten a few times so I didn't really see him as a problem. He was an old warhorse and that fight turned out to be a little difficult because he had fought a lot of tough guys in his career. I won by the split decision but, to me, it was hard because of his experience. Again, there would be quite a wait until my next fight. This time, I fought Anders Eklund at the Trump Plaza Hotel in Atlantic City and I knocked him out in the first round. My association with Dennis Rappaport would last until my fight against Everett "Big Foot" Martin in 1992, when we started another lawsuit. This time it was against Dennis, and Tom Moran was the driving force behind it; we were unhappy with Dennis because we thought we could have made $30m from a deal, but I think there may have been more to it than that.

Tom Moran was definitely an opportunist; any chance he saw to make money, he took. I really had a good relationship with Dennis, even though there were some flaws in the contracts for a couple of fights. There were some things that he did that were different, but Tom saw an opportunity to make money. There were a few reasons why we sued Dennis but, like I say, Tom was the one driving it and it took me a lot of years to realize that he was out for himself. There was one time down on Long Island when they tried to pay the judges off because the guy I was going to fight did not pass the EEG brain test to say he was fit to fight. There were also issues with money, but Tom was the greedy one. Admittedly, there was some legitimacy to suing Dennis, but I have to admit to being swayed by Tom too much. He was using me to make money; even though the money was mine, he knew it was going to benefit him, too. When I first met him, he showed me these young boxers; most of them didn't go to university or school, and he took advantage of them. He did help them, but he also helped himself.

Tom was always on at Dennis because the guy had a bad heart. Every time we would negotiate, he would start holding his chest and Tom would make fun of it afterwards. I didn't really like that. Dennis had a triple heart bypass, I think, so when we had negotiations, Tom would put the pressure on him and really push the issues. Dennis would have to stop and rest and take his medication, and later, when we walked out of the meeting, Tom would say to me: "He almost caught a heart attack that time." He would be laughing and I didn't appreciate that. Dennis would actually have to stop and take deep breaths because his heart was fluctuating when we negotiated. Tom would push and I really think Dennis gave us a lot of these deals because he knew Tom really didn't know how to negotiate. He would say to himself: "Well, this kid is going to blow the deal for Timmy, so I might as well give him what he wants." Tom would raise an issue and make a point of it because he knew he had the power to blow a deal for me. Rappaport would be thinking: "This guy is a young; he hasn't been in the game as long as me; I guess I'm going to have to give him what he wants." If Dennis knew that Tom was more experienced, he would probably have said: "To hell with you – get out of my office." He really wanted me to fight for him so he pushed the boat out to get me. He knew Tom was just learning, and that he was smart, and, like I say, I got a hundred grand each time we renegotiated. Every time I needed something, Dennis would sort it out, but Tom was better at negotiating than me and he would try to prove the point that he was stronger, better, and up and coming, but Dennis was a very wealthy guy.

Chapter Fifteen

Terrible Times

MY first fight of the 1990s was in January 1990, and it was the second in a row at the Trump Plaza. I fought Jeff Sims, who had learned to box in the jailhouse where he served seven years for manslaughter. He was the guy who famously split Ali's lip whilst sparring with him, and he had a devastating punch. In the jail, he had 21 first-round KOs, but I knew it was all about power with him. If you were able to survive the first two rounds, then you had a good chance of getting him. I remember that Dennis was in my corner. He was a good guy and I really do feel bad about the lawsuit, even after all of this time; maybe, if my mind was more focused back then, I would have stepped in the way and stopped it. Sims was one of Gerry Cooney's sparring partners, and so was I for a time; he was also a weightlifter. I remember, when I first walked into the Cooney camp, all of his sparring partners were all beaten up, including Sims. My first day with Gerry went okay; he would reach down on the left side and drill the left-hook wherever he wanted. The reason I lasted was because I was up and coming, and I wanted to be the champion one day like him. He broke all of them other guys up, and the reason why he didn't do it to me was because Slim was there with me. He let me go after four or five days because he couldn't figure me out. I had too much for Jeff; the referee stopped the fight in the fifth round and told him he was not going to let him take any more punishment, and that was it. He was strong and he got back up and he was mad because the ref had stopped it. He was swinging punches, but I was hitting him with too many shots.

Harold Smith was one of the most famous conmen of all time; it turned out he embezzled at least $20m. He was interested in taking me out to Indonesia. I first met him in 1980, when we were in California, training with Ali's amateur boxing team at the Santa Monica Gym. There were a couple of other heavyweights in there but Ali wasn't coming in that much. I was sparring with Eddie Mustapha Muhammad when he got out of jail. He was a light-heavyweight from Brooklyn, and we had some good battles. Harold was convicted in the 1980s for the biggest bank swindle in US history. He used Ali's name and set up a fraudulent company called Muhammad Ali Pro Sports. With the money, Harold wanted to take over boxing and he was paying fighters hundreds of thousands of dollars to fight in bouts at Madison Square Garden, and in other places, until they busted him.

Harold was stealing all of the boxers, who were all riding around in Mercedes, and, for a time, it looked like he was going to do it. It was after he went to jail and came home that I met up with him, because he came straight back into play. He was behind my fight with Greg Gorrell at the Bung Karno Stadium in Jakarta in March 1990. He called one of my people up and they got hold of me because he asked if I wanted to fight in Jakarta as he was taking a lot of fighters out there for a tour; Larry Holmes was going; the band Kool and the Gang were also going. I got paid $65,000. We got on the plane and flew out and I remember Ali was making everybody laugh because he was constantly doing magic tricks, for hours. I went to sleep and, when I woke up, he was still there, doing the tricks. We flew from Philadelphia to California; from California to Hawaii; then to Japan; then Bali, where Mick Jagger was married, before we flew to Indonesia. It took us 24 hours in the air. Larry Holmes was doing exhibitions out there with his sparring partners; Quick Tillis was there with some other fighters; Bernardo Mercado did an exhibition fight with Larry; and I was going out there to fight Greg Gorell.

We stopped at these Islands and the people there didn't know any of us, except for Ali – everybody knew Ali. We stayed in Jakarta for 19 days. I tried to get marijuana. I knew there was no drug testing out there. I went up to this Indonesian guy and I said: "Where can I get some marijuana?" He looked at me kind of strange, and then he just ran. I started chasing him and he just kept on running very fast. So, I went back to the hotel and I said to my people: "Hey, what's going on? I talked to this guy and I asked him to get me some marijuana and he just ran." My guy said: "Yeah, you can get 12 years in jail for just one joint. In certain countries out here, you can get the death penalty, so don't go asking people for marijuana." I also remember there was this club with a glass window, displaying about 100 women and you could pick any one you wanted. I didn't do anything, but some did; that's the way it was out there.

Greg Gorrell was tough, but he was small, and I kept telling him not to fight me because he was not going to win. If you remember, I had done this before when I knew the opponent was not in my league. Greg wasn't as good a fighter as me but he was a hard man. I told him to just try to make it look good and, if he came at me, he was going to get hurt, and he said: "Okay man." We got in the ring and he tried to fight me, so I warned him again. In the end, I had to hurt him because he kept coming at me. I was just telling him how to make easy money in this country without getting hurt. I won by TKO in the third, and I cut him really bad. I dropped him and he was bleeding and they stopped the fight. To me, he was just another opponent but he did not want to take the easy path.

Later, we were invited out to this big mansion house where they had a feast of food all around; it was like nothing I had ever seen before. There were tables all around the house with food and drink, including snails and lobsters. Everybody had a big respect for the guy that owned the place. He was a boxing promoter out in Indonesia and nobody messed with him. We had been watching a bout and, suddenly, one of the fighters started to elbow Greg Richardson, a bantamweight champion from Youngstown, Ohio, like an MMA fighter. He wasn't a regular boxer. He was kneeing and kicking Greg and doing other things not allowed in boxing. A couple of us ran up to the dressing-room, asking what was happening. I went up to the big man and said: "What the fuck is going on?" Then he looked at me and I caught myself. I thought: "Wait a minute, I'm howling at the guy who can get me killed" and I got kind of scared. He just said: "Yeah.".The referee was letting it go, so I went back into the dressing-room and I said to my people "I hope I don't get a bullet in my head" because I had disrespected the top guy and they don't mess around out there. Fortunately, he was cool with me, but he wasn't as tight with me after that fight was over. Before, he was really friendly, but that cooled off.

My next fight was in July 1990. We flew out to Seattle, where I fought Jose Ribalta. He was a Cuban guy who was a little bit tougher than me, but I thought I could knock him out because I had seen Tyson do it, so I didn't train like I should have. This was just a regular fight for me, something to get me further towards the title, but Ribalta came to fight and I suddenly realized this when he hit me one time. Again, I won a split decision. It was harder than I thought it was going to be; he could have won and upset me if I wasn't as clever as I was. I just wanted to win the fight and get on with the next, but I should have trained harder.

In March 1991, I fought Carl "the Truth" Williams at the Trump Taj Mahal in Atlantic City, and I trained pretty hard for that fight. I knew that he was a game opponent and he once could have upset Larry Holmes; he was close to winning and they gave Larry the decision. This guy had a good jab and he hurt me. I had to get in and fight; I had to chase and track him down – nobody wanted to get hit with my overhand right. He gave me a swollen eye and, in one round, I stumbled, but I fired back at him. It was a hard and intelligent fight. I had to think it out and he did the same; it was like a chess match. It was aggressive and I was on him every round, in his chest, putting pressure on. He hit me hard several times– in fact, he hit me so hard it took me ten years to remember it – but, in the end, I won because I still had the guts and determination, and I came out with the United States Boxing Association Championship title. It was my son Tim who called me up on the 'phone ten years later and said to me "Dad, I'm watching the Carl the Truth fight, and the guy beat the shit out of you" which is unusual because none of my children will swear in front of me. It was only then that I remembered who had hit me so hard; it had troubled me for many years.

My life had been on the downward curve for a little while now, and there were still more bad days ahead, but I was happy that I had not lost my touch, and my legs were still good. Losing your touch happens to a boxer, not always when they are too old and washed up; sometimes it happens when their head is not where it should be. I was blessed to be where I was; I just kept telling myself that. People could put me down and rip me off but nobody can cut off a true talent and, like I say, I had started out not believing I had it at all. The fact is you only get to become a contender for the world title if you are one of the best fighters in the world and I just kept telling myself that. I kept living my life, and looking after my babies, sometimes having a really hard focus to train properly, and sometimes slipping into depression and that downward spiral of drink and drugs that I'm sure some of you will be familiar with. I put enough aggression into fighting Carl, and the truth was that they gave me the fight on a split decision.

During this period in my life, I was deep into the process of suing Don King, so my days were filled with legal meetings, then off to training and raising my kids, and I had to try and keep my thinking right. It was difficult to keep your game; it was hard to see the horizon at some points, but I was damned if I was going to come out of this with nothing. During this time, my secretary, Eleanor, got a 'phone call, and she was told, if I got into the ring, I would be shot, so she panicked and she called everybody; she even called the police and said she had a threatening 'phone call. They called me and I got really nervous, and then, all of the sudden, my cousin summoned an army to protect me. He called his people and they came up and did what they do. They were all around me; he made sure nobody got near me. They were around the hotel and they had guns, but they were not aggressive or upfront; they were just there in case somebody tried something. I don't think there were guns in the arena because there were guards there, but I knew they were always close. Eleanor and her husband Bob were good friends; they were like family when I had first moved house up to Fairless Hills, another area in Philly. There wasn't that much killing and fighting there, and Pennsbury High School was rated number 14 in the country at the time. We raised our kids together.

As you can imagine, with all of this going on, I wasn't in the best shape of my life for my next fight, against Art Tucker towards the end of 1991. It took place at the Blue Horizon in Philly and was my first fight in my home town for 10 years, and somebody obviously wanted to unsettle me. I was overweight when I fought Art, but I won by a TKO in the third. Nobody realised that there were people in the audience with weapons. It was all pretty intense, but they made sure that I was protected. When you watch the fight, you can see that I was telling my guys to get behind me. I had the middleweight Greg Robinson and one of my brothers in my corner. I don't know why I was saying this to them – it was me they were after, not my friends – but, towards the end of the fight, you see me doing this. I was nervous because the threat was out there and I didn't know what was going to happen.

All of the shit that went on was crazy, but now, after all of this time, looking back at it all, I don't really bear Don King any malice. The way he ran his business is well known; everyone knows about Don. He was just a player, the top of the pile, and chances were given to me by him, from those early days of viewing him in the crowd when he was shouting "Tim, it's just me and you!", to being the Heavyweight Champion of the World. I loved the guy and, when he took me under his wing, I thought the feeling was mutual, and that we'd all earn our money and reach up as far as we could go. If things had been fair, we could have saved each other a lot of hassle but he didn't see me the way I saw him. I cannot say that he was behind the 'phone call to Eleanor, but it would have been a strange coincidence if he hadn't got to hear about it. At the time, it was a scary situation for me – I am a father; I've got my son Timmy Junior and I had daughters to think about, too.

Now, of course, I have Shanayiah, who is my youngest, and there are also Linnette, Mecca, Ayanna and Indya. Ayanna was born in 1988; I had her with Tammy, who went six months before she found out she was pregnant. She was the one that used to take the candy when we went to the store. Mecca was born in 1990, and there was also Tim Junior who was born in 1984, also children I had with Tammy. When she left me, I had to raise them by myself for 15 years. I had to cook, clean, cry with them; I had to do the lot of things with these children to try to keep their heads right, and I couldn't have done it without the help of my mom and my sister Rosalind. Tammy left because Indya was born and I never told her about it, on top of everything else that was happening. There I was, a heavyweight champion and I was a single parent trying to raise my kids. In the beginning, I used to go in the car with Mecca and she saw a bit of how depressed I was; I couldn't keep the act up 24/7. I know it was my own doing but it still hurt like hell; harder than any punch, swifter than any jab, it cuts you right through the heart when your daughter looks at you with tears in her eyes and says: "Daddy, where's Mommy?"

    I was the first to take Don and his son Carl King, who was acting as my manager, to court. I filed a $25m lawsuit on the grounds of fraud and conflict of interest and I really didn't know how much of that I was going to get. I had some good people behind me and I guess, when I sat down at the end of the day, when the kids were all in their beds and the house was quiet, I must have thought about what I could lose, although not so much my life, or any danger to my kids – there was that panic over the 'phone call and a couple of other things but I don't think anybody really wanted anybody to get hurt or anything like that. I just wanted what I was owed. I wasn't even 30 years old when we started the court case. I was coming into my prime, the best fighting years of my life, but I just couldn't go on the way I had been. I have mentioned the kind of money Don was giving me each fight, and it wasn't even a decent percentage. I was earning a good wage, but not the kind of money the Heavyweight Champion of the World was supposed to get. Larry Holmes had seen this, as had Ali before him; I got into the spider's web and I was trapped for quite a while. I could have gone on into my late 20s and early 30s, maybe getting the world championship belt again. I should have been financially secure and – who knows? – maybe the fight against Mike Tyson may have happened and, if I had hit him hard enough, I could have been part of writing a different history for the heavyweight championship. I was frozen out because of the court case, and it dragged on for years. I would sometimes lay awake at night, just thinking about it and all the stuff I had to do to be a father, a wage-earner, and everything else. In the end, I didn't even have the satisfaction of seeing Don beaten in the court. By 1992, I was at my wits end and pretty much broke. Don settled out of court for a million bucks, rather than risk going to trial, and that was the end of that. He had already moved on with Mike Tyson and nobody bothered me much. What happened to that money, and the way I wasted it, was my fault, my bad decisions, and me being way too trusting. It should have set me up for life, but it just didn't happen.

Chapter Sixteen

Pay-check Fighting

BY the time the court case had finished, I was 34 years old, and I was aware that time was ticking on for me as a boxer. I don't think I had any further expectations, other than making money, at that point, and I found out it was going to be impossible to have another stab at the title unless I knocked everybody out. Then who could stop you? When he was managing Gerry Cooney, Dennis Rappaport burned his bridges. The world heavyweight title had been won before by older fighters than me and, of course, afterwards, George Foreman won it at 45 years old. So, I soldiered on from one pay-check to the next. Talk of fighting Jimmy Lee Smith came about late in 1991, and the bout took place in Atlantic City in February 1992, about a week before Mike Tyson was found guilty of rape and sentenced to six years in jail. I knocked Smith out in the first, and I was feeling pretty good. When the news about Tyson broke, I guess perhaps a light did come on in my head for a little while about me becoming the champion again.

Tyson had been the unstoppable master-boxer until he was KO'd by Buster Douglas in 1990. I knew Mike's head hadn't been in the right place, but he was on his way back to the championship when all of this broke. It was bad for him, but it did pave the way for other fighters and, when he made a comeback four years later, I don't think he was the same person.

About six weeks after the Jimmy Smith fight, I was back in Atlantic City again to fight James Pritchard. He had lost his previous two fights against some pretty unknown fighters and I got the decision against him in the tenth, but I should have knocked him out. As I said, I was a working-fighter in my mind. Okay, I had the crazy notion that maybe there was another twist in the tale and a belt to be won, but I was just happy to be making money. Dennis was still paying us well and he was putting all of these fights together for me because he did have his heart set on me getting another shot. As a promoter, he was a good guy and he put his money where his mouth was but I didn't like the fact that he tried to get involved in the training side of things so much. I think he was just a passionate guy; it was like he was throwing the punches himself when he was telling me how to throw them to. He was good at what he did, don't get me wrong, but it was up to myself and my team to get me into shape for the fights. Like I've mentioned before, the hunger was no longer with me. In my early days, up and coming with Slim, if I had tried to dictate what was going to happen in training, Slim would have quit on me. Now, I had been the champ; I had the reputation; and it was me calling the shots in my camp because my coaches were on the payroll and there really was nobody to pull me back into line as a boxer.

I had stepped away from Slim, Don King, and all of those other characters but I think I lost some self-discipline during that transition. There was a certain amount of freedom to my actions. If I didn't want to train so hard, I simply wouldn't do it and there would be no repercussions for me until I stepped into the ring. I was doing just enough to get by, or what I thought was enough to get me the win and the pay-check. I think I would have quit then if I had the financial security my boxing career should have afforded me. Those two fights in Atlantic City were pay-check fights, and the one we had lined up next against Everett "Big Foot" Martin was in the same category, in my mind. He had lost his last nine and he was getting used to taking a whipping so I wasn't worried too much. I was spinning so many plates in the air in terms of being a boxer, a father, a businessman, and all the other things going on around me, I guess I just misjudged the situation.

The fight against Big Foot took place in Auburn Hills in Michigan. Dennis was there and he was saying stuff, trying to get people riled up, and he was telling me to do the same as soon as we got into Detroit about a week before the fight. We started bad-mouthing people. World Boxing Organization heavyweight champion Michael Moorer was there in the crowd, and there were other influential people, too. Dennis was trying to get some publicity and maybe get me another shot at one of the various titles that had passed from James Douglas to Evander Holyfield, Riddick Bowe and Lennox Lewis. I know he was trying to get me back into contention but sometimes when you do this kind of thing, it backfires. He wanted me to say stuff to Michael like "I'll knock you out in your mother's backyard out and put you in the hospital" and other nasty stuff. Doing anything like this is not in my nature, but that is what Dennis wanted me to do, to turn "Terrible Tim" into "Nasty Tim". The problem was that Auburn Hills loved Michael because he trained there, so we really put our feet in our mouths. I ended up saying all of this stuff to try and get the fight – I talked about his mom and I talked about putting him into hospital – and when I got into the fight against Everett, I was convinced I was going to beat this guy easily.

I thought that it was a close flight, but he was not in my league until he hit me. As the fight went on, I was starting to think that it was going to be up a lot tougher than I had thought it was going to be and I really wasn't in the best of shape. He kept on coming at me hard and strong and trying to win, which he did, on a judges' decision. Everything was really messed up and Dennis was really upset. I knew the defeat came from me blasting Detroit. We were there, training at James Toney's gym for about a week before and, as we worked out and went about the city, we were saying stuff to the people we met and steadily antagonising Big Foot because we wanted Michael Moorer for my next fight. It backfired because the officials knew I was saying all this stuff as it was all in the Detroit newspapers. They were wondering who it was who was coming into their city and bad-mouthing them, and in the end the judges gave the fight to Big Foot.

There was one more fight in 1992, against Tony Willis in Atlantic City in August, and I got the decision in that fight, but it would be another two years before I stepped into the ring again. I came back in August 1994 and I was feeling strong. My first fight was at South Padre Island against Sherman Griffin and I won by TKO in the third. I also stopped both Nathaniel Fitch and Jesse Shelby. I won in the first round against Jesse and I remember that, when I hit him, his eye-lids went up. I know I'm not the first fighter to mention that. It was like a sketch from a Tom and Jerry cartoon where the cat gets caught up in a roller blind whilst the mouse watches on with a grin. The only thing is, I wasn't the mouse on this occasion; I was looking for my way in. This was in March 1995, when you had Bruce Sheldon a month away from winning the WBA heavyweight title; Oliver McCall holding the WBC; and veteran George Foreman holding the IBF crown. I knew I could beat any of those guys. The fight against Shelby was in Philly, and I had the home crowd behind me, which is always a big factor for a fighter.

By 1995, I was doing okay, but I was still doing drugs here and there. Pancakes and syrup was a big thing, but I was also using cocaine sometimes, when it all go on top of me. The fall-out from the Don King episode lasted for a little while and, after all of that, I really didn't have the push to get myself in the best shape I could get myself into; and, of course, my age was now against me. Everybody was getting better opportunities than me, but Dennis was still looking out for me, which makes me feel bad because of how things worked out. I felt like I could have worked with Dennis after boxing and brought through some champions but, after the court case, that avenue was closed forever. My advisors found some little things in the contract, but maybe they were not big enough. I should have been looking out for my life after boxing, and what we did was wrong – he was going all out for me because he really loved boxing, just like we were trying to do with the Raiders of Boxing. I'm a big enough man to say I made a mistake with that.

I fought Jamaican Everton Davis in Phoenix towards the end of 1995, and I won in the seventh round by TKO. I was in shape for this fight. When I say "in shape", I was just about fit enough to win so I was still taking some chances in the ring, as well as, of course, with the drugs outside it as my fortunes and mood fluctuated. Tim Puller was next; he was known as "the Hebrew Hammer" and we are still friends today. I was ready for the fight and I trained hard for it because I heard he was doing the same. There's nothing worse than seeing an older boxing coming back and trading in on his name; if he can still do the business and entertain the crowd without doing permanent damage to himself, then I don't see the problem of people fighting on. In a perfect world, you should probably finish up in your early 30s with the money you made behind you, all ready to start a new life. Many of the greats went on too long, I think, but it's not always just for the money. Some carry on because they know nothing else. I think I would have happily walked away if I could have made a similar kind of money, or even half that money, doing something less demanding. Nobody knows when that blow to the head is going to happen which gives you problems in the brain. We all try to protect our heads and dodge them big old punches, hoping that everything is going to be alright, but, really, a boxer gambles with his future just for money and to entertain the crowd.

Tim Puller was a big guy, 6ft 6in in his socks, but I had too much for him, as I did against Alfred Cole, who, to his credit, took me ten rounds. Alf was a cruiserweight coming up, just like Evander Holyfield did, and he was trying to test the waters as a heavyweight. We fought at Madison Square Garden and this was an experimental fight for him to try and beat an old man like me. Again, I had to train really hard. I had to make sure because we knew, if he beat me, he had got himself a road to the title; they would pick the road to take him upwards; and I wasn't going to let that happen. I dominated the fight and, as a matter of fact, I broke my hand when I hit him with a left hook; I broke the bone they call "the boxer's bone". I was out of action for a couple of months but I kept on training at a high level for my next fight against Jorge Luis Gonzalez. On the same card at Madison Square Garden was my next opponent, Ray Mercer, who was beaten by Lennox Lewis. Evander Holyfield was also on the card and he beat Bobby Czyz from New Jersey. I stopped Jorge in the fifth round but I knew I could have trained even harder. What gave me a lot of motivation for that fight was my son Tim Junior, who was about 12 years old at the time; he led our entourage out to the ring.

It was rumoured that the winner of the fight between Ray Mercer and me would get a shot at the world title. I knew he had a hard jab and he was a game person, so I really had to ramp the training up even more for that fight. Again, I realized afterwards that I could have done more; as soon as the bell rang, I knew straight away that I was in for a hard battle. This was a young man and he was going to try and take my head off. All the time, he kept up the jab, and I have to say he had the hardest jab out of everyone I ever fought; his right hand had the ability to be devastating. It was a really hard time, and it was really competitive for me, just like a championship fight. I had known it was going to be a hard fight and that Ray was a clever boxer who had given a lot of people a hard time. I also knew, when I got into the ring, I didn't need to let somebody hit me because I had a good defence, and that's what saved me in a lot of my fights, so I felt, if I could just hang in there, I might get the chance to open up on him, which I did. When the final bell rang, I was convinced that I had won; and when they announced a unanimous decision for Ray, I couldn't believe it. Before the fight, I knew Ray had been robbed of a victory twice before, and they could have ruled with him because of that. I wasn't too upset, because that was the way boxing was; he was the younger up-and-coming fighter, and I was the old man. Ray even said to me at an awards dinner that he thought I had won the fight, but that isn't the way it was. He had said to me in the ring after the fight that it was his turn to be the winner now, and I knew exactly what he meant.

Chapter Seventeen

Ducking and Diving

BEFORE my fight with Levi Billups in November 1997, the HBO President Seth Abrahams told me I would be fighting for the championship if I won but, in all honesty, I was in no fit state to do that. Levi was an ex-American Football player who then got into his boxing like I did, and I knew he was another one coming up and trying to be the champion. He was trying to prove himself but I had too many skills to be beaten by him and I knocked him down three times in the first round. Then, about a month later, and a week or so before Christmas 1997, they sent me to Connecticut to fight Larry Donald at the Foxwoods Resort. Larry was trying to copy Muhammad Ali's style; he tried to box like him and he ran a lot during the whole fight. He outboxed me, but it was a close fight. I was supposed to fight someone else originally, and I told my promoter, before the fight, that I did not want to fight Larry because he moved too much. I would try to lean in and throw a punch and he wouldn't be there, so I didn't want to go up against him. I think HBO told me I had to fight him; they said, if I fought him, I would definitely get the title shot they had been hanging over me like a carrot on a stick, so I did it. He boxed really good and I lost the decision but, after the fight when I went and saw him, it looked like he had been beaten around the side of the head with a baseball bat. I really hurt the guy; he was leaning over and not looking very good at all.

The fight against Larry was the first of five defeats in a row, and I think this was when my body started to really show the signs of all the punishment I had put myself through. I was also using crack cocaine quite regularly, and there are not many sports people who make that stuff part of their training, but, like I say, I was just doing this for the money. My age was against me, too. I was two weeks away from my 40th birthday when I fought Larry, and I was starting to have real problems with my back. I did my best to get in shape for that fight, which wasn't easy, and I should have called it a day at that point in my career but I had commitments – people I did not want to let down, and bills to pay. Besides which, I'm a fighter and boxing is in my blood, even though I had lost a lot of the passion. It was all I had ever done, except work in that hospital, and, if had quit then, where would the money come from and what would be my future? I still felt I had something to offer. I could still attract fighters and people still turned up to see me.

After losing to Larry, a fight against Jimmy Thunder came up in Cherokee, North Carolina, in April 1998, and I was stopped again, in the tenth round. It was the seventh defeat of my professional career and Jimmy was tough. He was an American Indian and he'd fought a couple of tough guys and had done really well. I remember looking at him and I said to myself: "I can beat this guy." He was muscular and in real good shape, but I felt I could do it. I was training and sparring in North Carolina with Oliver McCall and Burt Cooper, two of the hardest punchers in boxing. They were whipping my behind to try and getting me in shape for that fight because Dennis Rappaport had sent me there to get me away from the partying and the drugs, but there was just as much of that going on down there. I was sparring with these guys every day and getting beat into shape but I had bad teeth – I had an infection – and I was taking antibiotics. Coming into the fight, I felt really sluggish despite the level of training I had done. Jimmy won the fight and you can tell, when you watch it, that I was not my usual self. I was taking the medicine leading up to it but the mouth infection was not going away. He won it fair and square; it was a close fight, even though I really didn't feel right. I think the judges and referees expected to see me do certain things in front of them and, if I don't do them, they are really disappointed, and that all goes towards losing because they expect more from me because of who I am. If they don't get it, if they are not seeing the real Tim Witherspoon, then they are going to vote against me. I'm not making an excuse here, I am just analysing my performance and why I lost. Yes, I know I had personal demons around me and, of course, these guys were younger and up and coming. On this occasion, the antibiotics set me back but I thought it was closer than what they scored.

Andrew Golata was number nine in the rankings and we were scheduled to fight in October 1998 in Poland. Golata had turned professional only five or six years earlier and he won 28 in a row until he came up against Riddick Bowe at Madison Square Garden in 1996 and was disqualified. He hit Riddick with a low blow in the seventh and, after that, a fight involving fans, corner-men and managers started out. The fight was shown on HBO and it ended up with around 20 people injured, 16 arrests, and a running battle inside and outside the ring. The whole thing was a mess. There was a crowd of over 11,000 people in attendance and there could have been fatalities. Things got so bad that even the Mayor of New York, Rudolph Giuliani, turned up after the trouble had calmed down to see what had gone on. The crazy thing is that Golata was winning when he started delivering the low blows and I don't understand why he did it and tarnished his unbeaten record. They had a rematch a couple of months later in Atlantic City and Golata did it again, and they awarded the fight to Riddick again. It caused a lot of publicity, but I would have rather of won the fight and gained something positive out of it, if I was him. He did get a fight against Lennox Lewis in the end and he was KO'd in the first. So I didn't know what to expect from Golata.

I was back doing a lot of drugs at this point. I was still partying, but I wasn't going out; I was doing it in my house, self-medicating, so to speak. Golata's manager, Ziggy Rozalski, came to my house a couple of times and said they could get me a fight and then they told me how much money was in it for me. I think it was at least $100,000. The second time he came was before the Press conference and I was upstairs, still coming down off of the crack from the night before, and they woke me up. Before I went down, I took a couple hits of crack and I wanted to hide the rest of it so I went into the clothes room in my bedroom, which was like a walk-in closet, and I put a chair in the middle and reached up. There was an opening in the ceiling and a small storage space above. What I saw there frightened me to death, and I would have put it down to what I was smoking, but I was not the only one to see it. There was a ghost-like image of a man standing up there and I asked him what he was doing. He didn't answer me, so I jumped down and I put some heavy stuff up against the closet door and ran downstairs. I decided to take my kids with me to the Press conference but their mother Tammy stayed at home – after my initial split with her, we tried again but it still didn't work out, When we got back, I went into the house and she was scared. I asked her what was wrong and she asked me to come upstairs. I started walking up towards the room and I saw that the closet door was open, although I had lent all of the stuff up against it so nobody could get out. I asked her if she had seen a figure up there and she said "Yes." We had seen the same thing and we both got really freaked out by it for a while, but we never saw it again.

I wasn't really training or anything at that time, and I'm sorry to say I was high on crack before the Press conference. I was also drinking, knowing that I had to go and stand in front of the media. I must have been crazy but that was where my life was at. The "self-medication" increased whenever things weren't going right, or I had a lot of stress in my life. When I came home from the Press conference, I started to train for the fight, but I really wasn't interested in beating Andrew; I just wanted the money so I could pay my bills and get high. We flew over to Poland about 20 days before the fight and we had some fun. The Polish are really nice and we met a lot of people. I was surprised because a lot of them were on my side and they wanted me to beat Golata, for some reason. The funny thing about this particular fight was that I knew he was an upper-cutter and, of course, I was expecting him to hit me low. He was aggressive, and I approached the fight by telling everybody that I thought he was a really nice guy. I kept using some psychology. Every time I met him, I was really friendly and I shook his hand and tried to talk the aggression out of him. I was in the newspaper talking really nice about him and I said that maybe he was having some troubles when he took the fights against Riddick Bowe. I think the way I approached the fight, and what I said to him, stopped him from using the low blows. He kind of respected me and he fought me with respect; there was no dirty play, and I didn't fight that way either.

We stayed in this hotel where the people could not do enough for us. There was, though, an incident with the Olympic boxer Johnny Bumphus, who had won the Golden Gloves, and another guy who was annoyed with all of the media attention surrounding Golata. We were all sitting there, eating breakfast, and Bumphus was standing up. The other guy must have been about 6ft 7in and he hit Bumphus – bam! Then he started to run away and everybody started chasing him. He jumped the fence, everybody jumped the fence, and then they caught him and we took him back to the hotel and said to him: "What the fuck are you doing?" He told us he had done it because he felt left out. This guy used to spar with Golata and he was so mad that he was getting all of the attention that he decided to hit Bumphus at breakfast to make some headlines of his own. When we thought he had calmed down, we released him but he just ran away again and we didn't catch him this time.

I fought in the Hala Ludowa in Wrocław which was a building that Adolf Hitler had spoken at, so the whole experience was a little bit chilling. It was still a great experience for me to be in Poland, and I learned a little bit about their culture and how they operated. Like I say, my heart really wasn't in it and I had no interest in beating Golata; I just went there to get paid. Andrew got the unanimous decision after ten rounds; I couldn't get him with the overhand right, even though I opened up his nose in the ninth. After the fight, I went and saw him in his hotel room and I talked to him a little bit and I asked him if he was okay. He told me that he was but then I saw a great big gash on top of his head, and I mean big. We stood around for a little while, then I wished him good luck and I left. Like I say, we had no trouble at all.

I was awoken once again from my slumber with the news of my next fight against Brian Nielsen, but the money wasn't so great this time. I was asked to go to Denmark to fight him and I said to myself "There's no way this guy can beat me." His people were allegedly paying people to take dives but I didn't know that until I got over there, and they ended up getting indicted for it. I met some of the promoters and they offered me the fight for forty grand originally. We flew in and I had my older brother Ralph and my good friend at the time, Leo Doherty, with me. Leo was an old Irish guy who looked out for me; he would come to my house and I would go to his and he would help me with my kids. My manager, Tom Moran, was also there, and when we flew in and met their guys; the first thing they asked was to keep hold of our passports and I said "No."

Initially, I said "okay" to forty grand. Then I went back to the hotel room and I had a think about it and I said to my people I wasn't going to fight him for a meagre forty grand. I think I'd upset my promoters back in the states a little bit by having this fight but they reluctantly agreed to me doing it without them. After we had checked into our rooms, I told my guys that I had a plan to get some more money; I told Tom to tell these guys that I was going to get sued if I fought because I was operating outside of my contract without the promoters' consent. The next day, I got up and I told them I was sorry but I couldn't take the fight and that we were going to have to go home because it was going to cost me more money if I fought. They said "Wait a minute", and they made a couple of 'phone calls and then they came back and said to me: "We will give you sixty grand." I said "I don't know, because there is going to be a lot of legal expenses", and my brother made out like we were getting ready to leave. As I said, they wanted our passports, and I wasn't having that, and then they came back again with $10,000 in $100 bills and I told them I would fight. I was delighted and I said to my guys that I'd got the price up, and we made around thirty thousand more than they offered originally. They didn't sue me when I got back home, either.

There was an agenda for the fight although I didn't know of any of this until I was stood in front of them and they were trying to take our passports. The plan was I would come out for the fourth round when the bell rang; they said to me to wait until Nielsen threw a couple of punches, then I had to throw up my hands and go down. It wasn't the sort of offer I could refuse. I wasn't even sure if Nielsen knew what was going on but I did exactly what they asked me to do. Before the fourth, we were going at it really hard for three rounds and I was hurting him. I knew I had to lose the fight or else we would not have left the arena in good health. So, the fourth round came and he was throwing left-right, left-right, and I went down. I got up and he threw some more and I was trying to make it look good as he hit me and then

I think they stopped it when I went down again. The first thing I heard after that was some woman shouting "Hey Tim, how much have they paid you to take a fall?" and I could hear the crowd booing. I felt bad about the situation, but my reliance on drugs, and the bills I had piling up, meant I needed the money. If I didn't do it, things would have been even worse for me. I felt bad walking the streets and people looking at me, knowing I was a cheat, but I just needed the money and that is why I took the dive. It wasn't a hard fight. I could have knocked him out if I had wanted to.

Before a lot of these fights, my back was starting to go out on me. Early in my career, I had cramps, which I think it were caused by an intestinal problem. When I stopped eating beef and pork items and started to cleanse, it got better, but, every once in a while, the cramps came back. I think I just needed to clean my colon, but I seemed to be getting the cramps every fourth or fifth round and I was getting tired of it. At the beginning of my career, Mark Stewart tried to get a specialist to check me out, but that didn't help; every time, they would be doubling me up in the fourth or fifth round. I think a lot of it was mental. I also think some of this was to do with using drugs. By the time I faced Greg Page in 1999, I knew that, if I didn't loosen my back up weeks before the fight, I would feel it at some point during the contest and it would tear me apart. It was something I couldn't get rid of unless I stretched and did sit-ups. It was hurting during the Brian Nielsen fight and I was really scared about it going out during the fight against Greg, which I was winning up until the point my concerns became real life. When the fight started, we were exchanging punches and I noticed something wrong with Greg. I hit him and saw he was motionless but I couldn't finish him off because of my back. I hit him a couple of times and I said to myself: "This guy does not need to be fighting any more." I saw the way he reacted, but I just couldn't finish him and he won the fight.

Greg died in 2009. He was only 50 years old. In 2001, he had fought against a guy called Dale Crowe, who hit him with a flurry of punches which made Greg slump into him. Crowe pushed him back against the ropes and he slid down to the canvas and was counted out by the referee. Greg suffered severe brain damage from that and there was pandemonium in the ring: 20 minutes passed before the ambulance arrived. Before the fight, Greg's trainer had complained to the commission about the lack of facilities, but he was ignored. At the emergency room, a CT scan revealed bleeding inside his head and he had to have brain surgery but he suffered a stroke and was paralysed down the left side of his body after coming out of a week-long coma. Greg's health after this was really poor. In the end, he slipped out of his bed and got himself wedged between the rail and the bed and wasn't able to breathe because of his body position. It was a terrible way for such a great man's life to end and I think this fight, and the one in Tottenham, England, between Chris Eubank and Michael Watson in 1991, started to make me think a little bit about the dangers of boxing. I was chasing the money so I could chase the dragon, and it was going to turn on me at some point and burn me with its fiery breath.

I fought Greg five years before these terrible events and whether I was seeing the early signs of this damage, or if Greg was just having a bad day, I do not know. We were fighting for a couple of rounds and then I saw him fading away. Between the rounds, they were trying to rub my back and get it going because I was in terrible pain. I said to my guys "I can't make this one, I think it is over for me", but every round they were saying "Try one more" so I tried to fight on but I knew that was the end and I gave him the fight. I wanted to go in and finish up but my back just wouldn't let me. Greg jumped for joy, and I was happy for him in a way – life was hard for Greg, too, he was another one who had to deal with Don King – and I told him he had done a good job, but I actually could have won that fight if my back had let me.

Chapter Eighteen

End of the Terrible

I WAS coming to the end of my professional career by the time I fought Monte Barrett at the Turning Stone Resort &Casino in New York. I'd fought six more times since I had lost to Greg Page, and I'd beaten Joe Ballard, David Smith, Dave Bostice, Elieser Castillo, Danny Wolford, and had my only ever drawn fight, against Mike Sedillo in April 2000. It was still in my mind that I could still kick most people's asses if everything was right with me, even though I was 43 years old. What I mean is I could still leap the physical and mental hurdles a fighter has to jump through to get himself ready for a fight. I knew I could beat Monte Barrett. We were on the undercard of the fight between Laila Ali and Jackie Frazier-Lyde, who are, of course, the daughters of Muhammad and Joe, and it took place in June 2001. Being on the undercard of a their fight, all be it the biggest billed one in the history of women's boxing, was a new experience to me, and I was really boxing more for a exhibition type of bout, than anything serious. The name Tim Witherspoon sat nicely on the card behind the main event, along with a couple of other champions and stars from recent history. I didn't train once again, not seriously, anyway. I had seen this guy fight and I figured I would knock him out in one or two rounds, so I didn't give him too much respect although I knew he had plenty of heart. I thought I could knock him out any time I wanted but I couldn't; he was there to fight. He represented himself well but I didn't think he won, although they gave it to him anyway. If you watch it, I think you will agree with me but, as we know, that is what boxing is about: it isn't always the best man who wins.

I fought Cleveland Woods next, at the Palace Indian Gaming Centre in Lemoore, California, in July 2001. Cleveland was a one-rounder; it was nothing, I went over there and – boom! – it was lights out for him. I did the same against Ed White in January 2002, but this time I didn't get paid when all that was keeping me going at this point was the thought of a pay-check. My glory years were behind me, but I could still put up a fight when I needed to. I was 45 years old and I knew I still had the ability to hurt people, but why was an old man still doing this to himself? My determination to go any further was pretty much exhausted, but the problem is that life gets in the way of your hopes and dreams sometimes. You get lost and caught up in it all; you get thrown out into the rain sometimes; and you are out there on your own. I had this big reputation, the whole world through. People liked me, and I had been in the champ of the entire world, as well as being associated with some of the greatest fighters of all time. If, at 21 years old, I could have seen my future, of course I would have done things very differently – even throwing the second Bonecrusher fight is something I may have reconsidered. My big payday never came; it should have done, but it was taken from me and I had to deal with that. At 45, I shouldn't have still been fighting for a pay-check; I should have been well off, with money in the bank; a good house; and taking care of my family. I do not fully blame Don King for all of the bad things that happened to me, and for the situation I found myself in, because I did have other opportunities come along. A lot of the wrong turns I took in the past, I take full responsibility for. I think everything that went on damaged me very much. When I became a contender, I thought I would have been taken care of, but I was sliced right up the middle.

The passion and the glory of the fight, and preparing for it, was in the past for me now. The ring and the gym was just my place of work; there was no more to it. When I faced Darroll Wilson in March 2002, I knew I could not continue for much longer. The time to hang up my gloves was fast approaching. My body was beginning to scream at me, and I was looking towards doing some permanent damage to myself. I fought Darroll in Vegas and he was a hard puncher. A young, hard, man hitting me time and time again was starting to hurt me bad. I was caught between the devil and the deep blue sea; living from pay-check to pay-check was all I knew. The thing about him was that he couldn't take anything on the chin and I finished the fight against him with a knockout in the second round without any real big damage to me. My back was seizing up and, if they had put me in there with one of the contenders with it as bad as it was, I could have really got hurt.

I was fighting under Dan Goossen, of the Goossen family of boxing promoters, by then. Dan was the one who managed the career of Mr T in the late 1970s, after discovering him. In the 1980s, the family started a company called Ten Goose Boxing and he was a really good guy. Darroll Wilson can punch and I did feel the power from him. He was short, strong, and muscular but I had to get him out of there because I didn't want to get knocked out myself. I had one more fight lined up in 2002, in May at the Silver Star Casino in Choctaw, Mississippi. Surprisingly, I was taken the distance by Ahmed Abdin, but I managed to win the decision. I'd had three fights in the space of five months and I had to seriously think about whether or not I should continue. Afterwards, I was given the chance to go up against Lou Savarese for the vacant WBO Intercontinental heavyweight title. That kind of made my mind up for me. In the back of my mind, I think I was realising there would be no chance of me getting a shot at the heavyweight title but Dan Goossen was really backing me, even though everything else was against me. There were younger guys coming through all of the time but, as a fighter, you never lose the need for the buzz, and perhaps the feeling of winning and soaring high up the ranks was something I was trying to replace with the crack cocaine. The taste of the gumshield in your mouth, or the sound of the crowd as you walk to the ring, is something you come accustomed to.

In our hearts, all us boxers are still young and in the prime of our lives, but nobody has ever repeated what Rocky Marciano did, 49 fights undefeated. So many fighters have gone before us and retired undefeated, and then the lure of the money to keep them in the lifestyle they are accustomed to comes creeping back at them when the bank-balance is running low. Sometimes they are seeking the buzz, something different from the general humdrum vibration of just existing without the gloves on your hands. As I said, I did not have the luxury, I always fought to live, day-by-day, week-by-week, and month-by-month. I wasn't an undefeated champion coming out of retirement for one last payday and to see if I still had the skills – I was putting food on the table for my kids. The fight against Savarese was in California and I really did slow down with the drugs for this fight. I wasn't using all of the time; I would do the cocaine to get high for a couple of days and then lay off of it. Against Lou, I had to quit because I knew everything was against me.

When I was at camp, I did not think about my bad habits at all, I would just train. It was when I was at home after fights that I would do it, but it wasn't like I was going out on to the streets and robbing people to get crack; that wasn't me. Everything was organised. I did it all cleanly and neatly and I didn't really go anywhere and do anything bad. I didn't bug anybody for money; I didn't tell anybody, I may have pawned a couple of things, but I kept most of my valuables. The training was nowhere near what I used to do. I really didn't prepare properly for the Savarese fight, and when I look back at it after all of this time, I really do feel bad because I was given a third chance to get the title but I didn't realise it. There were just too many obstacles and roadblocks in the way for me to overcome. When your mind is young and strong, and not worn away by the harsh realities I had faced, maybe you are better placed to turn the junk down. I had a house on the suburbs of the city and I was just doing my best to survive and get by. When Tammy left and I had been raising those kids by myself – with the help of my family, of course – I had to kept my habits away from them; they didn't see any of that.

The thing with Lou Savarese was that he was in tremendous shape and I heard him training, hitting the pads for four or five rounds. I was in the next room and I said "That can't be him hitting the pads", and then I realized he was training to hit me. I found out he had been in camp for six months, training for this fight, and I hadn't done anything. Instead, I was looking for the easy way to win – I was planning to knock him out in the first round, like Tyson had done in Scotland two years earlier. I do feel bad for Dan Goossen, because his heart was into putting me back on top for the third time, but I just wasn't into it. I tried to put up a fight. I gave Lou my best shot and then – boom! It was the first time in history I was properly stopped during a fight without going the distance; the other times, I had gone down and lost were for money, or to better my own life. I wish I could say I saw my life flashing before my eyes, but I didn't see any of that. I was a little off balance and it was a flash knock-down and the fight was over. It was over for Tim Witherspoon, too. I did not want to become an embarrassment. I wasn't trying to prove anything to anyone, and I was fighting maybe ten years after I should have quit and lived a nice life as a trainer somewhere with money in the bank.

Lou was a strong young man but, in the very beginning, I hurt him and almost had him out with my overhand right, as I had planned to do. But he survived it. That's all I thought I had left in me: bam! –try and take him out early, try to give him everything I have. He was hurt, but then he just started coming back – bang! bang! bang! – picking shots. When they stopped the fight, they didn't really have to. I was happy to carry on but I said to myself "Here's another sixty thousand bucks." Later on, I felt bad because the promoter was really in it to help me. If I could have got into shape, Goossen may have taken me to another championship fight, even at my age.

    The curtain fell on my 24-year career at Gulfport in the Grand Casino Pavilion, Mississippi. I can't say it was emotional or anything because I really didn't envisage it was the last I'd be fighting as a licensed professional. I'm still working out today, sparring and doing a couple of rounds of exhibition stuff for charity; nothing heavy – I'll be 60 in a couple of years. Boxing is in my blood, and I also try to pass on to the younger generation the stuff that Slim taught me, and how to defend. My last professional fight was against Brian Nix on March 15, 2003, and again I was defeated. I suppose, if I had have known it was to be my last fight, I may have felt a little bit emotional about it, maybe fanned some of those inner flames which had blazed right through me right at the start of my career and given me the will to win one more fight before the final bell rang. They were lofty heights I soared to, and nobody can ever deny me that. Without boxing, I guess I would have still ended up with the same kind of money worries, just without the fame and recognition. I don't have any regrets today – what would be the point? I've tried to help and guide boxers; tried to teach them about promoters and managers so they don't have to find out the hard way, like I did. That's what the Raiders of Boxing was all about, even though I don't think you will ever totally clean up the sport. It's hard; it's brutal; it can leave you injured, or even dead, without so much as health insurance or any kind of pension to help you in your old age if you do not have a good and honest manager. My professional record reads 69 fights, 55 wins (38 by knock-out), 1 draw, and 13 defeats.

I am convinced, though, that I did go out on a high. I believe I did beat Brian Nix (who used to spar with me; at one point, I knocked him out in training), but he won by the split decision, Again, I wasn't training because I thought I could just manhandle him any time I wanted, and I just didn't have the will to get myself into any kind of fighting shape. I would have probably fought again but I was watching other fighters of a similar age to me making fools of themselves in the ring. I was 46 years old and the time had come to end it; you had all of this young talent, all these guys coming up, and they wanted to make a name for themselves by hurting the former Heavyweight Champion of the World. I'd had enough and I decided it was time to concentrate on what I was going to do after boxing. You look stupid, coming back trying to become the champion again and trying to get your fights set up. At 46, and with my reputation, they would have probably tried to still help me but it wasn't going to work for me. I did try and get my license back, but then I just left it alone. They okayed me to do it but then I thought about Greg Page, and all the research into boxing and brain damage; there are a lot of things that can go wrong, especially when you're an older pro. You've got to remember, by then, you have been hit in the head for years and years and the next one could be the fatal blow. My mom said to me not to do it because it would be embarrassing and that is when I left it alone after weighing up all of my options. Eventually, I managed to put my own health before the cash.

When it was all over, it took some time to slow down, to reflect and look back at the past. My memories flip back to when I first started out, and, of course, to Linda. I just didn't want to take her into the boxing game because I knew it would destroy her – look what it did to me. There's the money, drugs and partying, and she was an extremely nice person who I wouldn't have wanted to bring down. She passed away a few years back. Linda knew my father before she knew me, and, in the beginning, really didn't like me because I used to joke around with her a lot. I went around to her house one day and we were just talking, and then I left and went home. She called me and asked me some questions and then we realized she knew my family. Then she slowly started to like me and I was happy, perhaps the happiest I ever was in my life despite everything I later did, and all of the places I went to in the world. She showed me how to be a gentleman when I was 18 years old. In the end, we just fell for one another. It feels like a lifetime ago now, and, in some respects, I guess it is. I still think about her, and about all of those times and all of the people no longer with us today. I think about Tommy Wade, and Slim Jim Robinson, and all of those who had a bearing on my career. None of us are here for ever; we leave our mark in the sand on some distant beach someplace and then that finally fades away. It gets washed out by the sea, or blown away by the wind. In the end, there's no trace of us being alive at all accept for maybe photos, journals, and films that record parts of our lives. For as long as boxing exists, there will always be a little place in its history for me, the first true Philadelphian to win the heavyweight championship.

Linda died of pancreatic cancer a few years back, but she never told me she had it. We split up years before, of course, and she had other children. Linette, the daughter we had together, told me, when I was travelling back and forth, that her mom was sick, but I didn't think it was going to happen that fast. I was in the UK when Linette told me I'd better hurry up as she didn't think she was going to hold on for very long. I had to get home fast – my friends John Murphy and Frank Bartley helped me make the arrangements – but she died five hours before I got to Philly. They say she was asking for me, but I was just too late and I think that will always haunt me. I was in the middle of something and I couldn't stay, so Linette had to make the arrangements to bury her mum on her own. I flew in for a while but I had other commitments and people who were relying on me so I couldn't be there all of the time. Linette took the news kind of hard and she had to raise the other kids after she had buried her mother; she had to do a whole lot of stuff. She made it out alright in the end; she did pretty good. She's a good kid and her mom would have been proud of her, like I am of all of my children. She came a long way from hiding under the bed from Larry Holmes and his bodyguards.

There are those moments in life that come along and knock the wind out of you, and I'm not just talking about in the ring. Despite all of this, I feel that I have been truly blessed. I can look into all the good and the bad that has gone on, all of the mistakes I made, all of the times I have been respected, disrespected, and punched in the mouth, but I am still here. I thank God for that, even if I don't have my mansion house and the financial security that boxing should have given me. I have my health and my children around me today. I have lived through the most terrible times, and come out the other side older, wiser, and still with enough energy inside me to keep going for a while yet, I hope.

Appendix: List of Fights

Oct 30 1979	JOE ADAMS	W	TKO	1
Apr 26 1980	ROBERT RITCHIE	W	KO	1
May 9 1980	ROBERT EVANS	W	UD	6
Jul 20 1980	CHARLES COX	W	KO	5
Oct 24 1980	OLIVER WRIGHT	W	TKO	2
Dec 11 1980	JAMES REID	W	KO	6
Jan 24 1981	ED BEDNARIK	W	KO	1
Feb 7 1981	MARVIS STINSON	W	PTS	10
Apr 11 1981	DAVE JOHNSON	W	UD	8
Jun 17 1981	BOBBY JORDAN	W	KO	4
Jul 30 1981	JERRY WILLIAMS	W	TKO	8
Nov 7 1981	CURTIS GASKINS	W	KO	2
Dec 5 1981	ALONZO RATLIFFE	W	TKO	7
Mar 20 1982	LUIS ACOSTA	W	KO	2
Jun 5 1982	RENALDO SNIPES	W	MD	10
May 20 1983	LARRY HOLMES	L	SD	12

Date	Opponent	Result	Method	Round
Jul 16 1983	FLOYD CUMMINGS	W	UD	10
Sep 23 1983	JAMES TILLIS	W	TKO	1
Mar 9 1984	GREG PAGE	W	MD	12
Aug 8 1984	PINKLON THOMAS	L	MD	12
Mar 3 1985	MARK WILLS	W	TKO	9
Apr 29 1985	JAMES BROAD	W	KO	2
Jun 15 1985	JAMES SMITH	W	UD	12
Sep 6 1985	LARRY BEILFUSS	W	TKO	1
Oct 12 1985	SAMMY SCAFF	W	TKO	4
Jan 17 1986	TONY TUBBS	W	MD	15
Jul 19 1986	FRANK BRUNO	W	TKO	11
Dec 12 1986	JAMES SMITH	L	KO	1
Aug 4 1987	MARK WILLS	W	TKO	1
Oct 14 1897	MIKE WILLIAMS	W	SD	10
Feb 17 1988	MAURICIO VILLEGAS	W	TKO	9
Jan 27 1989	LARRY ALEXANDER	W	SD	10
Oct 19 1989	ANDERS EKLUND	W	KO	1
Jan 11 1990	JEFF SIMS	W	RTD	5

Mar 12 1990	GREG GORRELL	W	TKO	3
Jul 19 1990	JOSE RIBALTA	W	MD	10
Mar 8 1991	CARL WILLIAMS	W	SD	12
Sep 10 1991	ART TUCKER	W	TKO	3
Feb 4 1992	JIMMY LEE SMITH	W	KO	1
Mar 23 1992	JAMES PRITCHARD	W	UD	10
Jul 21 1992	EVERETT MARTIN	L	SD	10
Aug 25 1992	TONY WILLIS	W	UD	10
Aug 12 1994	SHERMAN GRIFFIN	W	TKO	3
Dec 17 1994	NATHANIEL FINCH	W	TKO	6
Mar 24 1995	JESSE SHELBY	W	TKO	1
Oct 31 1995	EVERTON DAVIS	W	TKO	7
Nov 14 1995	TIM PULLER	W	TKO	2
Jan 12 1996	ALFRED COLE	W	UD	10
May 10 1996	JL GONZALES	W	TKO	5
Dec 14 1996	RAY MERCER	L	UD	10
Nov 4 1997	LEVI BILLUPS	W	TKO	1
Dec 13 1997	LARRY DONALD	L	UD	12

Date	Opponent	Result	Method	Round
Apr 7 1998	JIMMY THUNDER	L	UD	10
Oct 2 1998	ANDREW GOLATA	L	UD	10
Apr 16 1999	BRIAN NIELSEN	L	TKO	4
Jun 18 1999	GREG PAGE	L	RTD	7
Feb 25 2000	JOE BALLARD	W	KO	1
Feb 25 2000	MARK SEDILLO	D	PTS	12
Jul 8 2000	DAVID SMITH	W	TKO	2
Feb 22 2001	DAVID BOSTICE	W	TKO	1
Mar 31 2001	ELIESER CASTILLO	W	MD	10
Apr 13 2001	DANNY WOLFORD	W	TKO	3
Jun 8 2001	MONTE BARRETT	L	SD	10
Jul 29 2001	CLEVELAND WOODS	W	KO	1
Jan 18 2002	ED WHITE	W	TKO	1
Mar 10 2002	DARROLL WILSON	W	KO	2
May 18 2002	AHMED ABDIN	W	UD	10
Sep 22 2002	LOU SAVARESE	L	TKO	5
Mar 15 2003	BRIAN NIX	L	UD	10

Key: KO - knockout; MD – majority decision; RTD – retired; SD – split decision; TKO – technical knockout; UD – unanimous decision

Photographs

Page 111: Kevin Baker
Page 112: Tim Witherspoon
Page 113: Tim Witherspoon
Page 114: Tim Witherspoon
Page 115: Tim Witherspoon
Page 116: PA
Page 117: Tim Witherspoon
Page 118: PA
Page 119: Tim Witherspoon
Page 120: PA
Page 121: PA
Page 122: Tim Witherspoonon
Page 123: Keith McMenamin
Page 124: Tim Witherspoon
Page 125: Tim Witherspoon
Page 126: Keith McMenamin
Page 127: Keith McMenamin
Page 128: Kevin Baker
Page 129: James Buckland Photography
Page 130: Greg Lambert